ROCK CLIMBING

⟨ **W9-BLN-262**

ROCK CLIMBING

A TRAILSIDE GUIDE
BY
DON MELLOR

Illustrations by Ron Hildebrand

A TRAILSIDE SERIES GUIDE

W. W. NORTON & COMPANY

NEW YORK   LONDON

Trailside: Make Your Own Adventure is a registered trademark of New Media, Inc.

The text of this book is composed in Bodoni Book with the display set in Triplex
Page composition by Eugenie Seidenberg Delaney
Color separations and prepress by Bergman Graphics, Incorporated
Manufacturing by South China Printing Co. Ltd.
Illustrations by Ron Hildebrand

Book design by Bill Harvey

Library of Congress Cataloging-in-Publication Data

Mellor, Don 1953 —
Rock climbing: a trailside guide / by Don Mellor;
illustrations by Ron Hildebrand
p.   cm. — (A Trailside series guide)
Includes bibliographical references and index.
1. Rock climbing. I. Title. II. Title: Trailside make your own adventure III. Series.
GV200.2.M45   1997   796.52'23—dc21   96-52821
ISBN 0-393-31653-X

W. W. Norton & Company, Inc., 500 Fifth Avenue, New York, N. Y. 10110
www.wwnorton.com
W. W. Norton & Company Ltd., 10 Coptic Street, London WC1A 1PU

3 4 5 6 7 8 9 10

796.522
mε

CONTENTS

F O R E W O R D

At *Trailside* our aim is to offer more and more Americans an alternative to the stressed-out, high-speed electronic world we call modern "life." Our need to counter the effects of the fast track makes us search for ways to nurture our minds, bodies, and souls. We yearn for a slower, more sensible pace and a gimmick-free, natural place to which to escape. That search, along with a growing consciousness of our environment, has awakened an avid interest in outdoor adventure among people from all walks of life, of all ages, and from every corner of the country.

Trailside: Make Your Own Adventure was born of this return to the outdoors. As a how-to television series for outdoor adventure, we strive to guide the uninitiated by providing reliable, useful, inspiring information; true incentives to get out and "make your own adventure." For the trail-wise or those considering a new activity, we provide advanced techniques presented by seasoned outdoors men and women who crystallize years of experience into accessible, practical advice. By increasing the ranks of outdoor adventurers, we hope to contribute to a larger family of advocates for the preservation of open, wild places.

Climbing the South of Heaven route, Rattlesnake Canyon, Joshua Tree National Monument, California.

Active outdoor pursuits are nearly as diverse as their participants. People are taking to trails, seas, rivers, lakes, rock faces, caves, summits and canyons, glaciers and jungles. To safely, comfortably meet the challenges they seek, outdoor enthusiasts employ an array of special gear, from classic canoes to the latest in hi-tech titanium bicycles. We try to stick to explaining what you *really* need, what works best in the field, and how to use it. At *Trailside* we remain focused on making every adventure appeal to people who never thought they could do it. To fulfill that promise, we tackle a broad range of activities in both our television shows and our books, and make our technical instruction as accessible yet comprehensive as possible, infusing hard information with inspiration and plenty of encouragement.

Our mission is to guide a new community of adventurers to the pleasures of the outdoors. Our responsibility is to ingrain in those newcomers a respect for the natural world. We urge everyone venturing outdoors — whether in the wild or in an urban park — to follow simple guidelines to ensure that your trail or back-country or down-river experience remains for others to enjoy in the future. "Leave-No-Trace" guidelines are woven into the fabric of every Trailside Guide and every television adventure. These rules are simple yet profound in their effectiveness; they will enhance your experience and preserve open spaces for others. Basic "no-trace" rules include:

- If you packed it in, pack it out.
- Travel and camp in small groups.
- Camp at established overnight sites.
- Always camp at least 200 feet from any stream or pond.
- Respect other adventurers; travel quietly.
- Take only pictures, leave only footprints.

Get out there and make your own adventure, but, please, do your part: leave no trace of your passing.

— *The Editors*

WELCOME

I made my first rock climb on a 50-foot cliff by a pond in the New England woods when I was a sophomore in college. Bill, our student-instructor, lowered a rope from the top of the ledge and, peering over from above, described to me how to tie a bowline by wrapping the rope once around my waist. I fumbled the rope into something that looked like a knot, and another beginner peeked over my shoulder and said something reassuring like, "I think that's right," while Bill goaded me upward by telling me how easy the climb was. (I surmised later that he had been named "instructor" of this motley group because he was the one who had climbed before.) I was terrified, but the higher I got, the more committed I felt. I was sure that Bill wouldn't be able to hold me if I fell, and so it was a struggle for my very life. When I dragged myself over the top, I was breathing so hard that the ground spun, and it took ten minutes for me to gather the strength to stand and walk back to the security of the woods, pledging to heaven that I would never — *ever* — try something like that again.

During a recent climbing trip almost 25 years later, I found myself in a new and different world, crouched on tiny footholds about 40 feet up and looking out at a huge

Peak fall foliage and a sheer drop below: Jeff Achey climbs a steep crack in New York State's Adirondack Mountains.

seemed endless. I clawed my way over the lip and clipped the top anchors, hyperventilating and dizzy, recollecting that I'd had this feeling before.

The years between my first struggle on New Hampshire granite and my recent odyssey on plastic in New York have been packed with climbing. (Yes, I did break my pledge.) I've dangled with feet cut free on overhanging sandstone in Tennessee, stood balanced on the tips of strange granitic Needles in South Dakota, jammed the spectacular vertical crack on Katahdin's Armadillo Route in the wilds of northern Maine, awakened to the surreal pink landscapes in the high Utah desert, and spent nights slung in a thin nylon hammock on the 3,000-foot face of Yosemite's El Capitan.

My life has been shaped by the sport. My friends, my career choices, even my choice of residences have all somehow been constructed around climbing. This book welcomes you to begin the journey, confident that you too will be changed by the experience, but hoping, of course, that your start will be safer than mine.

overhang. No quiet pond lay in the distance. Instead of the chirping of birds, all I heard was hard music pounding in from speakers all around. I was in lower Manhattan at the amazing Chelsea Piers complex, site of one of the country's newest and best indoor climbing walls. Below, one of the facility's instructors held my rope. "It's easy," he coaxed. "I train by going up and down this one three times without stopping." That was all I needed. I swallowed hard and headed out, lunging for bizarre plastic shapes — blue, yellow, and red blobs — like huge mutated mushrooms and cauliflowers. My arms burned and the overhang

BEFORE WE START

Sports like climbing can be learned only under the watchful eye of an expert teacher. Such a book as this is not intended to replace personalized, expert instruction. Instead, it will introduce you to the fundamentals of the sport and accompany you as a reference guide as you gain proficiency and wisdom. Its chief aim is to provide you with sound basics, not to elaborate on the more complex systems that you'll learn as you grow more independent as a climber.

Climbing can be dangerous. Let's get this fact up front right from the start. Climbers who have had long safe careers are alive today because they understand the risks and behave

Your goals will be to acquire good physical technique and a thorough understanding of the equipment.

accordingly, not because they are lucky. Most climbers don't place their sport in the same category as other so-called risk sports, like bungee-jumping or hang-gliding. Instead, they see their game as one of control, of mental and physical achievement.

They don't toss their fate to the winds or play variations of Russian roulette.

Someone who is new to the sport and who can't fully understand the variables can be in a most perilous position. Yet there seems to be a predictable learning progression — sort of a bell curve — that describes the relative danger that accompanies climbers as they mature. Their first days out, they are super-safe: They won't do anything without thoroughly checking their systems to make sure that everything is in order. Then, I'm afraid, some climbers gather too much confidence, they begin to view the game as easy, and they let down their guard. This stage often lasts until the climber has a close call, reads about a disturbing accident, or simply grows up. Whatever its source, a new attitude takes over, bringing with it a safer approach and a more mature acknowledgment that the risks are huge and that climbers must be ever-vigilant. My advice? Skip stage two.

Read this book closely, practice its techniques in a controlled setting (you'll be surprised by how much you can set up in your backyard), and continue to ask questions. Establish

DID YOU KNOW
The first ascent of El Capitan, the Americas' tallest and sheerest face, took a total of 47 days spread over a period of 17 months ending in 1958. The current record for the same route is under 4 hours.

good habits. Become a safe climber, and you'll never be short of partners. In addition to all that you'll read here and learn from others, your most trustworthy tool will always be your own common sense.

Why We Do It

Watch a child at play and you'll know why people climb. There seems to be something innate, even primal, about our desire to clamber up trees or boulders or walk nearby hills. Some say that it comes from our simian forebears: We are genetically pro-grammed to swing from the branches of trees to gather food or to escape danger. Others claim that we enjoy climbing simply *because* it is risky. Our ancestors thrived by successfully facing daily perils. Now that our environment is tamed, we still feel an urge to put ourselves in precarious positions to fill the void left by the disappearance of the saber-toothed tiger and the other hazards of the wild.

Although such an argument might also explain our attraction to roller coasters or downhill skiing or scary movies, most climbers would probably deny the anthropological explanation, arguing instead that it just feels good to stretch our muscles and to see the world from on high. Whatever the source of our desire,

Glacial silt from the Canadian Rockies gives Lake Louise, in Alberta, its characteristic hue. Settings like this inspire climbers to explore the wild places.

The innate urge to climb may not be universal, but for those who possess it, the impulse comes on in childhood, when every tree or wall must be climbed.

drawn upward toward apparent peril, and, at the same time, we want to survive.

This dichotomy is the essence of climbing. Success on a hard climb is immensely satisfying. To struggle, to doubt, even to suffer for some moments — these activities block out the rest of the world and inspire us to focus on one goal, perhaps as intently as we've ever focused on anything else in our lives, and when we come out of that tunnel, we are in many ways changed. When you feel your fingers begin to melt under a steepening bulge of rock and you focus like a laser on the saving handhold above, you won't be balancing your checkbook in your mind or worrying about your next term paper. No, you just

it's there in many of us.

Mankind is a risk-seeker, but more valuable to his survival is his desire to live and be safe. Put a baby on a table, I'm told, and she'll crawl to its edge and look over, but she won't jump. Climbing's allure lies in these paradoxical urges: We are

want one thing — the handhold —
and when you get it, all is right with
the world.

Climbing's therapeutic value
has long been recognized. Outward
Bound, for example, has been a
model for countless programs that
stimulate personal growth through
the challenge of climbing. You've
seen the picture: The nervous
beginner is locked on to a rappel
rope and trembles at the edge of a
cliff. The instructor's job is to make
that person take the step, to trust the
system and herself so much that,
once she's done it, she will be able to
face the other challenges in her life
with renewed confidence. In the
Marines, it goes something like this:
"Move it, dog breath, or I'm going to
push your sorry butt off!" At Camp
Good Grief, in New York's Adirondack Mountains, where children are
brought together with counselors to
understand how to face the world
after the death of a parent, when
climbing the instructor clips in
alongside the child and, together,
they slowly lean out into the void.

Climbing is a metaphor for life
itself. There is the aspiration and the
uncertainty, the journey and the risk,
the success and its concomitant satisfaction. Life on the wall becomes a
simplified model of life in the harried
world, a model with equal anguish,
but one whose challenges are carved
into perfect definition. We win here
and we know that we can win else-
where.

Who

One of the wonders of climbing,
which few other games can share, is
its inherent fairness. You don't have
to compete against anyone else or
even follow a book of rules pre-
scribed by others. It's just you and a
steep surface. In a way, climbing provides its own handicapping system.
The highly-trained athlete and the
overweight office-bound businessman
can suffer the same agonies and feel
the same elations. The daughter and
her dad can share the anxiety of
rubber soles slipping on rock and be
gratified to know that perseverance
pays off. In short, there's a climb for
everyone.

Climbing isn't exclusive. Learn
properly, choose your challenges sensibly, and you'll continue to amaze
yourself. I've seen climbers as young
as 3 and as old as 83, climbers who
are blind or in other ways handi-
capped, climbers who have spent
their lives on city streets, and
climbers who grew up tramping the
rugged hills. There was a time when
climbers were mainly oddball types,
scruffy outcasts who lived a life mis-
understood by the mainstream. Today,
however, that's all changing. Climbing
is riding a crest of popularity, and
Americans are growing accustomed to
seeing climbing on television and pictured in commercials.

Perhaps most significant in this
boom has been the proliferation of
indoor climbing walls. Almost every
one of the country's metropolitan

Indoor walls have changed the face of climbing forever, making it one of America's fastest-growing adventure sports.

that make it worth the struggle. You'll find camaraderie with new friends with a shared purpose, you'll learn respect for a vertical world you might never have noticed otherwise, and, best of all, you'll make discoveries deep within yourself.

Where

In most people's minds, rock climbing takes place on the steep rock walls of high mountains. Certainly, this has been the traditional realm of the game, a pursuit that began eons ago as man scrambled to high points in search of game or to build dwellings safe from attack. It isn't clear when he began climbing just for fun, but with the advent of nylon ropes and more advanced gear, he was able to figure a way up even the most uncompromisingly vertical rock faces, and *rock-climbing* became a specialty within the activity of mountaineering.

areas has a climbing wall. And so do universities, high schools, grade schools and sports clubs.

This book will bring you into the world of climbing, guide you to proper instruction, show you what you might accomplish both indoors and out, and examine the relationship between these two worlds that seem so different but that at their hearts are really one and the same. At first, and in either setting, the challenge will seem daunting and the gear too technical. But with your early successes, you'll find rewards

No longer seeking simply to get to the top of a peak, but instead looking for sheer physical difficulty, climbers took their game away from the mountain areas and found good challenges on smaller crags and boulders, in urban areas, and in the flatlands far removed from the mountains where the sport began. When climbers first set up their ropes on these shorter walls, they were probably preparing for, or fantasizing about, a trip to the real mountains. But it wasn't long before the short climb became an end in itself. In fact, some of today's best rock-climbers have never even been to the high mountains.

The first artificial climbing walls were crude training devices, hand- and footholds glued or bolted onto plywood or concrete walls for no other reason than to build the strengths needed for *real* climbing. Who could have predicted that in a few years the artificial wall game would evolve

Skills learned indoors or on smaller practice cliffs are applied to the most spectacular settings, like the Dragoon Mountains of Arizona.

into a sport of its own? Much like mountaineering's descent into the flatlands in search of practice areas, rock-climbing's move indoors and onto artificial surfaces began as training but has since become a world unto itself.

Your first steps upward may be in the gym, on an artificial wall of strange surface angles and over-hangs, dotted with colorful plastic handholds; or it might be outdoors on a natural cliff. Neither is more valid or satisfying than the other, and nei-ther precludes your merging the two games as you develop as a climber.

Whatever your start, the basics of rope work and physical movement are the same. What you learn in one setting will be fundamentally useful in the other.

GETTING STARTED

The safest way to learn, of course, is from an expert and attentive instructor. You might have perfectly capable friends who are willing to show you the way, but too often such informal instruction won't focus on your needs as a beginner. Camps and outdoor groups frequently offer such climbing courses, but to keep the costs down, some depend on good-hearted volunteers. That might work well for Little League, but watch out in the vertical world.

Over the last decade, climbing guides and instructors have developed some professional networks that have led to much-improved teaching methods and standards. The American Mountain Guides Association, for example, is a growing organization

TOP-ROPING VS. LEAD CLIMBING

Climbing is done two basic ways: *top-roping* and *leading*. The difference between them is shown here. The top-roped climber (right) is *belayed* by a partner on the ground who keeps the rope snug to the climber, pulling it in as he climbs and locking it off if he falls. Out-doors, the rope is set up beforehand by a person walking around to the top of the cliff via a non-

of individuals and climbing schools that share information and work to establish standards of practice for the profession. Certification and accreditation by such an organization is a good way to measure the competence of professional instruction.

Mountain guides are a fairly independent lot, however, and can be wary of any intrusion of bureaucracy. Some excellent guides and guide services refuse to be a part of any organization. If you do use a guide or guide service that isn't accredited, you might get an idea of its experience and professionalism by asking about the following:

- Insurance
- Medical qualifications
- Land-use permits for the areas used
- Client referrals
- Guide training and experience
- Accident records
- References from other professionals

Overall, the networks established by guides' organizations have been

technical route and anchoring it, either to trees or to mechanical anchors set into the rock. In the gym, the ropes remain set up from rings bolted to the top of the wall.

The *lead* climber (left) begins on the ground with no pre-established rope from above. She simply climbs, trailing the rope, and running it through *protection* she sets into the rock at intervals to shorten the distance of the potential fall. She's still belayed from below, but, as she climbs above her highest anchor point, she risks a much longer fall. For this reason, lead climbing is done only by experienced climbers. Once the lead climber reaches the top, or a good ledge within the length of the rope, she anchors herself and belays her partner from above. The *belayer* then becomes the *second* on the rope, removing the protection as she follows the rope-length, or *pitch*.

very good for the consumer. Look for such networks and standards to evolve and improve.

If you learn indoors, you'll notice that some of the procedures differ from those learned from outdoor climbing guides or even from those in this text. The gym world is new indeed, and gym managers continue to shape their methods to make them as safe and simple as they can. Gym instruction is generally geared toward use of a particular facility; don't infer that you are being trained for the Eiger North Face when you learn your knots beneath a towering sheet of plastic. In fact, most gyms do a responsible job of defining for their clients what the gym *isn't*, and they strongly encourage getting enhanced training before heading outside.

Experience itself is the best teacher, but there is a wealth of supplemental information out there to help you along. Instructional guides like this one are essential to aid your understanding. Another, called *Mountaineering: Freedom of the Hills*, has been a kind of climbers' bible for many years. Its focus is on overall mountain skills — compass work, first aid, and glacier travel, along with rock-climbing — but its information is simple and sound. It belongs on every climber's bookshelf.

Magazines are also useful, offering tips on technique that you'll find helpful as you move forward. Instructional videos cover much of the same material, but these have the advantage of being able to show climbers in action, not just in heroic poses. And predictably, climbing has even reached cyberspace. When I heard two clients of mine discussing the nuances of a particular knot based on what they'd heard on the "net," I realized that, at least for me, the wilderness was no longer just the forests and the mountains. It was the whole electronic world opening up everywhere and enhancing the games we play outdoors.

HISTORY AND CULTURE

Getting into a new sport can be like entering a new culture; with climbing the emphasis should be on *"cult."* But don't be put off by its unfamiliarity. You'll quickly pick up the language and the ideas, the gratifying commonality of experience that ties climbers together like no other group. This chapter is an overview of the sport to help you become acclimated. I hope that it not only puts basic climbing into a context, but that it also gives you a feel for the antecedents from which present practices have evolved. Today's climbing makes more sense, I think, when you can see where it has been.

The sport has come a long way since the early days, when climbers simply tried to get to the top of the mountain rather than deliberately tackling the peak's most imposing sheer face. There were no rules or laws other than those natural ones described by Newton. As the sport grew and technologies allowed us to climb virtually anything, climbers imposed limitations on themselves to keep things sporting. Predictably, there will never be complete consensus as to what these limitations should be. And so as climbing thrives, so do a number of schools of thought on how it should be done. Let's look at some of those schools.

In so doing I'll begin to use

On big walls like El Capitan in California's Yosemite National Park, artificial, or aid, climbing is often the only way to go. Progress is made by standing on nylon stirrups attached to pitons driven into thin cracks.

feet (or chin, knees, elbows, whatever it takes) to get up the route. The rope is used only to save him if he falls. It isn't used for upward progress. If the climber hangs on the rope or any other gear even only to rest, then the climber has not climbed the route free. One could take the issue to extremes, arguing that shoes and gymnast's chalk or even pants are artificial aids. Generally, however, you can claim to have done a route free if you start at the bottom and end up on top without having weighted the rope or any gear.

climbing terms — the jargon of this particular sport. Such words appear in italics; definitions for them can be found in the Glossary, page 179.

FREE VS. AID CLIMBING

A climb is *free* if the climber ascends the rock using only his hands and

A climb is *aided* or *artificial* if gear is used for upward movement. The aid may consist simply of grabbing a carabiner as a handhold, or it may mean an entire climb spent hanging in nylon foot stirrups dangling from hooks or pitons, with the climber never once actually grabbing the rock with his hands. Aid climbing is uncommon, and you needn't worry about it as you start; its use is generally reserved for big walls that aren't otherwise climbable.

Whether a route is aided or free-climbed doesn't necessarily matter to anyone except the climber himself unless when making the aid ascent, he damages the rock by pounding in pitons where others haven't needed them. It's also considered bad form to claim to have *done* a climb, implying that you did it free, when actually you grabbed a bit of gear or rested on the rope.

An aid climber in action, dangling in nylon stirrups from anchors wedged into cracks.

TRADITIONAL VS. SPORT

Traditional climbing refers to the practice of leading a route from the ground up, without inspecting it from above or placing any anchors while hanging on the rope. Its pleasures come from solving unknown problems, cleverly working out protection anchors to make the climb possible, or simply going without safe anchors, relying instead on courage and self control. Traditional climbers claim that this is real climbing, with all of its adventure and its risks. There is a lot of gray area between this approach and the next. Some "traditional" climbers do inspect routes from above, and some after having fallen, leave the rope clipped to the highest protection, instead of pulling

it back to make a pure ascent next try. Such "transgressions" are forever the stuff of debate.

Sport climbing refers to lead

DID YOU KNOW
One of America's most famous landmarks, the dramatic 900-foot Devil's Tower in Wyoming, was first climbed in 1893 by two pioneer homesteaders. They spent six weeks driving stakes into the vertical cracks and fashioning a ladder to the top, just in time for a flag-raising, Fourth of July celebration on top!

Snowbird, Utah, hosts one of scores of competitive sport climbing events held around the world.

centration is on sheer gymnastic movement, often pushing the limits of what's physically possible and doing so without big risk. To a sport climber, the physical climbing moves are the goals themselves, and the route might be achieved only after having its harder sections practiced on a top-rope. The achievement comes when, after all of the falling and hanging and inspecting, the climber makes it to the top in a single push from the ground without a fall, making what we call a "redpoint" of the route. In many ways, it's like a choreographed performance.

GOING WITHOUT THE GEAR
Bouldering

Many climbers hone their skills on short walls or boulders, rocks so low that they can jump off or fall without

climbing done with the security of pre-placed protection anchors (usually bolts) and a knowledge of what's up there before starting out. The con-

text continued on page 29

THE RATING GAME

Some climbers, like other athletes, seem bent on having their feats recognized, even when they might claim to be in it for the pure joy of movement. "Aw shucks, it was nothing." Translation: "It was extreme 5.13, and the magazines had better get it right." And so if achievements are the stuff of

recognition, or if we want be able to recommend a route to someone else, we need a system for describing the relative difficulty of a particular climb.

The most basic element of the system is the numerical grade given to a route. Stay with me here; it's not as bad as is looks. Early climbers used the most elementary rating system:

CLASS

1 = Rough hiking.

2 = Steep scrambling.

3 = Steep, unroped, hazardous climbing.

4 = Roped in sections, often moving together over varied terrain; the rope is employed only on the tough parts.

5 = The climber has a stationary belayer, and the climb is so hard that protection must be set between the climber and the belayer to reduce the length of a potential fall.

6 = Aid climbing.

We are concerned here with climbing in Class 5. As climbers sought to further delineate the difficulties of their ascents, there emerged what they called the Yosemite Decimal System. It broke Class 5 down into decimal increments: 5.0 would be the easiest and 5.9 would be the limit of human possibility. In 1952, Royal Robbins boldly assigned that futuristic 5.9 grade to a route called The Open Book at Tahquitz Rock in southern California. Over the following decade, all the hardest routes were called 5.9, and then 5.9+ for the really outrageous ones. Climbers, it seemed, were stuck on mathematical logic rather than truth in advertising when they were grading their routes. 5.10? Why, the number doesn't even exist. Finally, in the early '70s, climbers took the cap off the grading system, and 5.11s, then 5.12s, and so on were established.

Note as you get into the sport that the climbing areas with a longer heritage stick to more conservative grades; they adhere to the older ideas that were the norm when the system was capped. Newer areas and younger climbers feel more at liberty to attach high numbers to their routes. A route rated 5.6 at the Shawangunks in New York State, for example, might be 5.7 or 5.8 at West Virginia's New River Gorge. Such discrepancies might confuse some people, but as the sport grows increasingly homogenized by traveling climbers, the grades will probably grow more consistent. Until then, the debates over grades for a particular route will continue to give us something to do in the off-season.

Here is a vain effort to describe a very subjective system: 5.0 – 5.4 Easy. Though the climb is definitely difficult enough to warrant a rope, most people in good condition could get up these routes even without specialized footwear.

continued on page 28

5 . 5 - 5 . 8 The general inter-mediate realm. Such routes require rock shoes, and only someone with unusual athletic ability could climb a 5.8 first time out.

5 . 9 - 5 . 1 0 Harder still. Requiring a thorough under-standing of technique and good finger strength. Remember, 5.10 was reserved for the elites only a few years back. At this level and above, climbers attach a letter (a, b, c, or d) to further delineate the grade. 5.10a is quite a bit easier than 5.10d.

5 . 1 1 a - 5 . 1 1 d Some recre-ational climbers might be able to top-rope such a route after many attempts, but only a very skilled climber can lead 5.11 traditionally.

5 . 1 2 a - 5 . 1 2 d We are get-ting into elite land.

5 . 1 3 a - 5 . 1 3 d Climbers here have devoted themselves to training, and even the best usually spend many attempts in order to succeed.

5 . 1 4 Introduced to Americans in 1988 by Frenchman Jean Bap-tiste Tribout. Only a handful of American climbers have achieved it, and virtually no one can get such a route first try. 5.14s are status routes that see many (often hundreds) of attempts by the very best climbers before they succeed.

5 . 1 5 And returning the favor to the traveling French, American Chris Sharma climbed the world's first 5.15 on a limestone cliff back in the homeland of Tribout and company.

Gym grades are still evolving, with many gyms developing their own systems. Some do use the decimal system and assign number grades to indoor routes, but since the medium is different, the grade evaluates different qual-ities of a climb. Typically, the gym grade reflects more arm strength and endurance and the outdoor grade reflects more technique and footwork. Gym climbers often find themselves discouraged when they try to compare numbers, and like-wise, outdoor climbers often get spanked by the unrelenting over-hanging nature of the modern indoor routes.

Don't put too much emphasis on grading as you start out, espe-cially if you are making the transi-tion between plastic and rock. When you move from indoors to outside, humble yourself a bit, and start low down on the scale until you begin to understand the sub-tleties required of climbing on real stone.

Practice the craft in safe settings. Traversing back and forth low on a rock face is an excellent way to learn footwork, handholds, and other climbing techniques before venturing up.

text continued from page 26

risk. Boulders provide an opportunity to practice moves too difficult to attempt when you are leading high off the ground. It has evolved to become almost a sport within a sport, and some of the best find full satisfaction in doing the moves low and safe. Boulder routes are called, ironically, boulder "problems," and the solutions to such problems can be fiercely difficult. Even so, such a safe environment is a good place to

THE NAME OF THE GAME

Since climbers can use various methods of preparation and practice to get up a route, terminology has evolved to describe the relative "purity" of an ascent. Perhaps all this doesn't matter a fig to you; if not, just go out and climb. But I'll include it here because you'll inevitably be listening in on the discussions as you join the world of climbers.

ONSIGHT: The climber leads the route first try with no prior inspection.

FLASH: The climber does the route first try but may have had

continued on page 30

some tips from others.

BETA: Information, tricks to help you to figure out the moves required of a climb. From "Beta-Max" — as though the climb is on tape.

RED POINT: The climber leads the route after having worked on it in practice. The term came from the Germans, who would paint a red circle onto the rock at the route's base when it had been climbed using some aid. Once the route was climbed bottom to top without a hang or a fall, the circle would be filled in: thus the red point.

PINK POINT: The gear and carabiners are left in place as the leader does his so-called free ascent. This is becoming the norm on the hardest routes, and many climbers are starting to call this a red point.

YO-YO: A variation of the traditional theme. The climber may fall, but if she does, she lowers to the ground, leaving the rope in place as she rests for the next attempt.

HANG-DOGGING: The climber hangs on the rope after a fall in order to rest. Technically, he has made all of the moves free, but the climb as a whole must be considered an artificial one.

WORK: The process of learning a route on a top-rope or leading with falls and practicing the moves. One might decide to "work" a route before trying a red-point.

I could go on and on with this list of terms that further define the climb. Crazy, isn't it? Sometimes you'd think that climbers would rather talk than climb. There's a great T-shirt out there that puts forward a popular sentiment. It reads, "Shut up and climb!"

---

extend your reach.

What is the safe height that you can boulder? That depends on how far you are willing to fall (and how controlled you'll be) and what kind of landing is below. If the ground is uneven or strewn with rocks, you could break a leg falling only a few feet. It's getting more and more

common for boulderers to use *crash pads*, large squares of foam, much like oversized sleeping pads, to cushion their landings.

Crash pads can help, but more important, you should have a skilled and alert *spotter* any time you are getting into the risk zone. Spotting a climber is much like spotting a gymnast: you can't actually catch the falling climber, but you can control his landing. When spotting a fellow climber, keep both hands up and tuck your thumbs into your palms to reduce the risk of thumb injury as you receive the climber's weight. Typically, you'll catch the climber from behind, just under the armpits, keeping him upright and absorbing the impact of the fall. A really good spotter is rare. Climbers don't practice it enough.

Free-Soloing

The climber who simply climbs, without the benefit of a safety rope and free from the dangling gear, is said to be *free-soloing*. It is a practice, however, that doesn't make much sense to most climbers. Falling means dying, and nothing justifies such a risk. Every so often, we read about good climbers who have fallen to their deaths while free-soloing, even on routes that have been well within their ability. But there are just too many variables: A handhold could break, fingertips could "sweat" off a move, the climber could even be startled off a route by a bird or a bees' nest.

Many beginners who have read about free solos, where the hero climbs hundreds of feet relying only on his cool and his fingertips, think that this must be the ultimate expression of the sport and something to aspire to. It's interesting to note, however, that most of the free-soloing I

An alert spotter takes much of the risk out of bouldering, and is a reminder that climbing is built on trust.

DID YOU KNOW
Patagonia, the outdoor clothing company, began when climber Yvon Chouinard started making pitons. As his climbing gear gained a following, he put out a line of stout canvas shorts designed for the rigors of climbing. It wasn't long before a whole line of apparel followed. Today, Patagonia donates a percentage of its earnings to environmental causes, "rent" to the planet.

At Smith Rock, Oregon, *To Bolt or Not to Be* was a revolutionary climb by Frenchman J. B. Tribout that led to greater acceptance of pre-protected routes on the American climbing scene. Shown here is Stephan Glowacz.

must be some self-imposed limits on what we consider fair play. Rock climbing in the United States has long been influenced by the British, who imposed very strict rules on the sport. British climbers once scorned the use of pitons or other technological aids, saying that they brought the climb down to the level of the climber rather than inspiring the climber to rise to the challenge of the climb.

see out there on the cliffs is being done not by the experts of myth, but by beginners who haven't matured enough to acknowledge the dangers.

ROCK CLIMBING'S ROOTS

Take a power drill and a supply of construction bolts, and you can "climb" any rock face in the world. Big deal. For the sport to thrive, there

Two of America's most influential climbers were Californians Royal Robbins and Yvon Chouinard. Both were profoundly impressed with the British ethic, and both in turn passed this influence on to American climbers. Robbins was a prolific writer as well as a first-rate adventure climber. His was the first solo climb of El Capitan, for example, and his thin paper-bound *Basic Rockcraft*, published in 1971, is the most influential instructional guide the country has seen. It describes climbing as a craft of ingenuity, in many ways a spiritual experience, and it firmly sets a standard to which climbers have aspired. Chouinard's influence came from his manufacturing of gear. It was Chouinard who endorsed and enhanced the British idea of using chocks instead of pitons (chocks wedge cleanly into cracks as anchors; pitons are violently hammered home and subsequently damage the rock). In the early 1970s Chouinard created two classic chocks, the Stopper and the Hex, and his 1972 gear catalog was a treatise on "clean climbing." By the end of the decade, few climbers even owned pitons.

In the days of pitons the biggest sin of all was deliberately altering the rock. The expansion bolt, permanently set into a pre-drilled hole, was seen as a curse, and climbers in America were united in their belief that a proliferation of bolts would be the end of the sport as they knew it. Climbers went to great lengths to climb without resorting to the drill. In addition to the newly-developed chocks, they used metal hooks on sharp ledges, nylon slings taped onto spikes of rock, and all sorts of clever anchor devices that left no trace on the rock as they passed. Most respected of all was the climber who laid his life on the line to climb some blank section of rock without any anchors at all, where a fall would be

his end and where only the best self-control would bring him safely to the top. Such a climb and such a climber would be at the top of the game.

During the 1970s and early '80s, the world looked to the Americans as leaders of the sport. The great walls of Yosemite were revered, and the climbers who scaled them were models abroad. But this changed. While American climbers were growing comfortable with their position, others, particularly the French, had chosen to dispense with some of the rules to push the standards up to the next notch. In many ways, it was inevitable. The rock of the American cliffs is naturally cracked and allowed for the placement of the clean anchors we were developing. Many of the crags of Europe are limestone — steep, pocketed, but without cracks. Such cliffs simply wouldn't be climbable unless they were protected by preplaced drilled anchors rather than chocks.

DID YOU KNOW
During World War II, the U.S. Army used Seneca Rocks, West Virginia, as a training ground for mountain troops. So busy were they that one wall still bears the name "Face of a Thousand Pitons."

The Europeans took things further. Not only did they protect their routes from above, but they also began rehearsing them on a top-rope, and, sin-of-sins, would hang on the rope to rest between attempts. In the United States, this was unheard-of. We thought that if you fell, you must lower back to the ground for another sporting attempt.

Climbers, as you'll see, are number-conscious. Although many of us claim to be in it for the pure joy of climbing, most become very heated when discussing the numerical grades assigned to their routes. Many climbers are more likely to describe a route as a "5.12" than as a "beautiful crack." As the Europeans changed the rules, they improved their grades and their gymnastic skills. When they brought these to the United States, the impact was revolutionary. Consider two cutting-edge achievements done in America by outsiders. First was Australian Kim Carrigan's success on a new Yosemite route. The Aussies had just whipped us in yachting, and he left us with a climb called America's Cup and a challenge, "You can have it back when you get good enough." Shortly thereafter, Frenchman J.B. Tribout visited Oregon and climbed the hardest route to date in America, giving it the unheard-of grade 5.14. and a name that said it all: "To Bolt or Not to Be."

Smith Rock, Oregon, site of the French invasion, became increasingly known for its bolted face climbs, and across the country, blank and otherwise unprotectable routes saw lines of bolts as Americans tossed out the gospel of Chouinard and Robbins and embraced the European methods that led more efficiently to the higher numbers.

For a period, the "trads" would complain bitterly about bolts, even removing them in some areas, claiming that such routes had been stolen by unfair means. Sport climbers responded with impressive achievements, and gradually, their unclean methods became a standard for many climbers. The controversy is not quite over, and the sport continues to evolve. Perhaps, however, the chasm isn't so deep. The best sport climbers are taking their impressive gymnastic skills onto the higher remote faces and achieving some amazing traditional ascents, and even die-hard traditionalists can occasionally be seen in the gym or on a sport route, knowing that it will not only improve their strength and skill, but that it will also be a whole lot of fun.

Whatever their superficial leanings, climbers continue to share fundamental values. Environmental damage is wrong. Graffiti is vandalism. Litter is a scourge. Safety is vital. You'll hear more about the "great debate" when you hang around the gym or the crag, but I urge you to do your part to make sure that these important values and behaviors endure.

M O V E M E N T

Watch a skilled climber at work. She flows effortlessly up steep terrain. Foot placements are sure, strong hands cling to sharp holds, and her whole body seems comfortable, loose, and light. She is a vertical dancer whose choreography comprises a sequence of pulls and pushes, of high steps and balanced foot switches. It looks easy, and you are drawn toward the wall to try it yourself.

From your new perspective, however, the wall is steeper and the holds less positive. You grunt and heave and throw yourself toward what looks like a small rest ledge, but you are disappointed to find that it slopes dishearteningly downward. Your foot

skates, and your forearms burn. You scream for your belayer to snug the rope, and you sit back in your harness, wondering what magic that climber must possess that let her float so easily to the top.

After only a few climbs, you'll see that it isn't magic at all, but the application of some simple principles of movement, concepts that aren't especially difficult to understand or to master. Granted, much of what you'll do on the vertical will be intuitive: Everybody knows how to climb a tree. But when you add to this some new ideas about efficient movement and body position, the handhold that seemed so tiny before becomes quite

Attentive and deliberate footwork is the foundation of all climbing technique.

my lessons by giving my students just enough information about the system to be safe, and then I turn them loose to climb, without lengthy or specific instructions. After a while and once they've gotten their feet wet (or more fittingly, their knees scraped), I begin to give them *ideas*, not directions. A good teacher won't dictate a route by pointing out hold-by-hold sequences. Instead, he'll describe concepts, broad ideas about how one moves on rock. This teaching approach not only focuses on the most important elements of the technique, but it also allows the newcomer to solve the problem in front of him by creatively putting those concepts to work.

BASIC PRINCIPLES

CLIMB WITH YOUR FEET Your legs contain your most powerful muscles; almost all upward movement comes from leg power, and almost all resting occurs from finding an efficient stance. The most useful comment I can make to a struggling beginner is, "Look below you. The answer is in your feet." Note also that small steps are usually more efficient than long ones.

LOOK AROUND This probably sounds too obvious, but, once on the rock, it's easy to become so focused on the terrain above that you miss key pieces of the puzzle right in front of your body, or even hidden by your body as you lean too close to the wall. Lean out, survey what's avail-

useful and the sloping ledge is actually fairly accommodating. This chapter introduces you to the movement of climbing. We will put aside for later the technical wizardry of fancy gadgets, and we'll focus on the best climbing instrument of all, the amazing human body.

Climbing technique isn't learned by listening or reading; it's the result of doing, making mistakes, experimenting, and reflecting on how the process works. As a climbing instructor, I limit specific instructions at first, confident that experimentation is the best teacher. I begin

able. Maybe the solution is off to the side. Perhaps it simply requires stepping up onto a foothold only inches above your present stance. Remember, the world will look different from even the smallest change in perspective. Experts can interpret the landscape and visualize body positions from below. As a beginner, you'll have to experiment.

FIND POSITIONS OF BALANCE AND REST Relax. Take your time. If you are tense or off-kilter, you'll grip too hard and quickly lose strength. Rather than lunging upward, look around, shift your body position, lean off to one side, or shift your hips. Experiment with positions that allow you to rest. You'll be amazed at the creative rest positions you'll discover, and, when you've mastered the rest, you'll be fresh to take on the section above. Good climbers are good resters, even on overhanging rock.

USE BONE, NOT MUSCLE Let your skeleton bear the load. Muscles are good for short-burst contractions but not for endurance runs. Hanging from a straight arm beats hanging from an arm whose muscles are contracted. With an open hand grip and a straight arm, you'll be able to keep your strength longer and get it back faster when you're tired. Look at photos of climbers in action and note their straight-arm hangs.

Learning to Rest

One of the best possible training exercises is to climb back and forth

Annie Whitehouse demonstrates perfect rest position on Wyoming limestone: arm straight and hips in, transferring weight to her feet.

along the bottom of a wall (keeping safely just a few feet from the ground) until your arms are burning with fatigue. Then pick a random location and stay there for as long as you can. You'll discover that there are really two rest positions needed at each stance: one to rest your right arm and one to rest your left. As you hold on with one arm, you'll be able to dangle the other and gently wiggle your fingers, letting the blood, and with it the strength, return. An appendage held high is quickly drained of both. Figure out what the two rest positions are, and think about how they work.

What are your hips doing? Subtle shifts and tilts here can make a huge difference. Bring your hips in to rest and out to move upwards.

text continued on page 40

As you get into more specific techniques, you'll begin to see that most moves share one idea: opposition. Almost every trick you will learn to keep glued to a vertical surface involves somehow exerting two opposing forces against each other.

Figure 1 shows a *layback*. The climber's feet stick because his hands and arms are pulling while his feet push in the opposite direction. If the climber were to stand up straighter and reduce the inward force supplied by his arms, his feet would quickly skid off.

Figure 2 shows the crack-climbing technique known as *jamming*. Once again, the climber relies on the opposition of forces. The hand (or finger or foot or whole body) stays in place because pressure is being exerted against both sides of the crack. The concept applies in a fingertip crack just as well as in a body-wide *chimney* crack.

Figure 3 shows the undercling, which is really an inverted layback move. Useful holds need not all be right-side-up. Look how the undercling helps keep the climber's feet in place and at the same time allows her to extend her reach. By pulling hard enough, the climber can keep her feet stuck even to a featureless wall. Note also that such a hold uses the climber's biceps muscle in a powerful position.

Figures 4 and 5 show body position while slab climbing. The climber on the low-angled face does, in a way, use opposition (Figure 4). He lets gravity pull him toward the rock, and he keeps this force as near to 90 degrees as possible. Look what happens when another climber (Figure 5) leans into the rock for that high handhold: The forces cease to be opposed, and the feet slide.

Opposition can be combined and applied in creative ways. The climber on the left is "jamming" and "laybacking" at the same time, while the climber at right is cleverly exerting pressure with his thumb against the opposite wall of the crack. Sometimes (below) a controlled lunge — for a moment there is no contact with the rock — is necessary to make that long reach.

text continued from page 37

Which muscles are engaged? A beginner typically contracts every muscle in his body in the struggle to hold on. Think about this. If you use only those muscles that are needed, the rest of your body can relax. Your breathing will slow down, and the strength in your quaking arms will gradually return. Be patient enough to discover the position that works.

Be Creative

The climber's maxim used to be "keep three points of contact on the rock at all times." We were also told to "remain in balance and keep movements smooth and controlled." Finally, we were admonished: "Never use your knees." No wonder we didn't get anywhere. Rule number one: There are no rules about technique. If it works, it works. Granted,

Practice the open grip. It's not only effective, but it reduces stress on the finger joints. It's also the way our primate forebears use their hands when climbing.

you'll soon get to know that some approaches are more *likely* to work than others, but don't worry about style points. The best climbers are innovators, pioneers whose moves were once called bad technique by their contemporaries.

There are times when a lunge will work better than a controlled reach, a knee is more secure than a foot, and one point of contact (even no points of contact!) might be just what you need to make the desperate connection to the hold above. I've used my chin to rest, my forehead for leverage. I even remember biting onto a tiny flake of rock for balance while I switched hands. You can use your elbows splayed like outriggers for stability, your butt for a devious side-rest, your shoulders to hold you firm against a corner. If you've got it, use it.

A CLOSER LOOK
Hands and Fingers
So much for broad concepts. Let's talk about the specifics.

The photographs accompanying this section will help you understand the many ways you can use your hands to climb. There are a few different ways you can grab a simple handhold. Note how an *open grip* hold transfers the load to the skeleton and engages much less hand muscle than the normal grip you'll start with. The open grip takes a little time to get used to, and it won't work in all situations, but it belongs in every climber's repertoire.

HANDHOLDS The *crimp*, or *cling*, grip for smaller holds seems logical enough, but consider what it does to the finger joints. Use it only when nothing else works and lay off if you

Two variations on the crimp grip. The tiny hold (top) forces the climber to over-stress his finger joints. A newcomer risks injury by subjecting his fingers to such forces. The climber below has stacked his thumb over his forefinger, adding strength to the hold while reducing stress.

feel any pain. Consider in its place a *thumb stack* over your first two fingers. This is kinder to your joints, and it adds quite a bit of power to your grip.

Handholds, both on real rock and those in the gym, come in every shape imaginable, so you'll have to adjust your grip for each hold to take full advantage of it. Experiment here, feeling the hold gently at first as you try this or that position before finally locking onto it.

Some climbing moves require

using only one or two fingers. Do not expect your neophyte digits to be able to perform here. The specialized strength required takes years to develop, and if you ask too much of your fingers, you're flirting with injury. If you do choose an extreme one- or two-finger hold, try to keep your fingers straight in the open grip position, hanging from bone as much as possible.

JAMMING Used in cracks, the hands and fingers are usually better as jams than grips. Fingertips slotted into a "bottleneck" (a narrowing) in a crack can be surprisingly solid. Sometimes, you'll need to enhance the wedging by cleverly exerting pressures outward onto the sides of the crack, but such a jam is much less secure than the bottleneck slot. If the finger-sized crack is parallel without obvious constrictions, try jamming with the little finger up, elbow at a right angle to the crack. If you pull the elbow in line with the crack, the jamming becomes *camming*, fundamental to thin-crack climbing.

The most solid hold of all is the *hand jam*. A skilled climber with a well-placed hand jam is virtually anchored to the cliff. One good hand is the equivalent of a rest ledge to such a climber. The hand jam works like a big cork in a bottle-top. Find a crack that narrows at its base, put your hand in loosely (thumb usually pointing in the direction of pull), and tense it up by bringing the "meat" of the thumb muscle into the palm of

Jamming is essential to crack climbing. 1) Finger jams in a thin crack. 2) When the crack is a bit too wide for secure finger jams, you must find less secure finger stacks to hold on to. 3) The hand jam is employed in somewhat wider cracks. Note that the jam is most secure when the thumb points in the direction of pull. 4) The end-to-end hand jam, or fist jam, is used in cracks too wide for a hand jam. Don't tuck your thumb into your clenched fist.

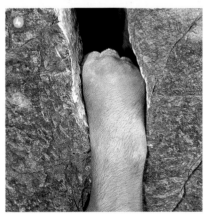

the hand. If the rock is coarse or your hands are tender, this move can be rough on the back of your hand. But otherwise, when properly executed, this placement can be as secure as any.

If the sides of the crack are par-allel and don't provide the natural constriction of a crack that narrows at its base, you'll have to create the outward exertion of forces necessary to hold your hand in place. The bunching up of the thumb muscle under the palm, or any other way you

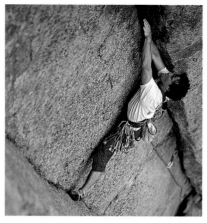

This climber (left) is jamming a thin crack while at the same time stemming a wide section with his feet. The route is on Wyoming's Devil's Tower, famed for its unique columns that require such stemming technique. Classic chimney technique (right): Guide Ed Palen demonstrates the security provided by straight arms pushing his shoulders hard against the opposite wall. He keeps his hands low for maximum holding power while his legs provide upward thrust.

can spread the hand to exert force onto the walls of the crack, will suffice. One point to remember: *You are climbing with your feet.* The jamming described holds you in place while your feet push your body upward. Keep this firmly in mind and your jamming technique will quickly improve. Note: The steeper the crack, the more effective it will be to "upslot" a low hand jam with the thumb pointing upward in the direction of pull. This acts like an undercling and greatly extends your reach.

Arm Bar

Chicken Wing

The dreaded "off-width crack" is too wide for hand jams and too narrow to wriggle the whole body in. Crack climbers rely on two techniques for such a problem: With the "arm bar" (left) you create pressure against the walls of the crack by tensing your biceps and working your palm against the back of your upper arm and shoulder. The "chicken wing" (right) is a bit more contortionist, but really locks the climber in place. Note that footwork is still essential here.

ADVANCED JAMMING

Certain sizes of cracks fit a climber's hands and fingers; once basic technique is mastered, such cracks are easy and secure. The between-sized cracks are most difficult. Climbers will refer to such cracks as "off-fingers" or "off-hands" or "off-width." These cracks are climbed by advanced jamming techniques adapted to the various sizes of cracks. The off-fingers cracks can be

Climbing a chimney at Joshua Tree National Monument in the high desert of southeast California. Climbing any crack requires keeping the forces working in opposition at all times.

used by means of creative *finger stacks*. The off-hands cracks can be climbed by using a clenched fist held endwise against the sides of the crack. Note that for a typical hand jam, the fingers are held open and not closed into a fist. Think about the bone damage you'd incur if a hand

jam slipped. In an end-to-end fist crack, the hand can be clenched without such risk to the fingers.

Cracks from around six inches and up to the width you can actually slither into require either an *arm bar* or a *chicken wing jam*. Both will hold you in place, but both require

Two uses of the foot for face climbing. Edging (top left) requires a high heel and a stiff foot. Using the toe, as shown, requires strong feet and stiff shoes; it's better to use the side edges of the shoe. When the terrain is sloped (bottom), bend your foot and point your heel downward, bringing as much of your shoe's sole into contact with the rock as possible. A climber's feet (top right) are carefully inserted into a crack and torqued to provide security.

jammed feet and legs to provide the upward push for climbing.

CHIMNEYING Any crack you can actually fit into is called a *chimney*. The *squeeze chimney* is just that: a crack so narrow that you have to slither upward by squeezing and struggling (and grunting and groaning). Not a happy activity. As the crack size widens, you'll be able to bridge across between the walls (remember the principles of opposition) to make headway. In all cracks, think of yourself as an inchworm. First the top half of your body moves up and locks in, then the lower body scrunches up for the next push. The lower half does the work; the upper half holds you in place once you've gained some ground. Move both halves at the same time, and you're on your way down.

The perfect finger-sized or hand-sized crack is a joy to climb. The hands feel locked off while the body leans out and pushes hard on secure feet. Cracks that don't lend them-

In wider cracks, the heel-toe jam provides the necessary opposition.

selves to good jams, however, can be real struggles.

Your Feet

I sometimes say that *all* climbing is in the feet. Yes, that's probably an oversimplification, but it's a concept to keep in mind. Most of your weight is on your feet, almost all resting occurs as you transfer weight to the feet, and your feet and legs are by far the strongest team in your body. Take advantage of them.

VISION Most essential in developing your footwork is vision: Learn to see the subtle rugosities (wrinkles, creases, texture) offered by the terrain and the rock. In most climbing gyms the footholds are colorful blobs bolted to the wall and are therefore obvious — not too much thinking required here. But on the newer more sophisticated molded indoor walls, and especially on real rock, there is a wealth of footholds that beginners don't notice. I remember during my first season as a climber walking under Airation in New Hampshire's White Mountains, then one of the East's hardest routes, a thin crack on a granite wall. I couldn't for the life of me imagine how anyone could climb such a route. It was vertical and as smooth as a parking lot. Years later,

when I got my second look at the route, it had been mystically transformed. The crack was wider, the rock less steep, and footholds were everywhere. Magic? Plate tectonics? No. It was vision. I had simply learned to see what had been there all along, and when I finally climbed the route myself, I found it fairly straightforward, with ample footholds and rests along the way.

FOOTHOLDS Once you've identified some potential footholds, you must decide how to use them. Look at the photographs of feet in action (opposite). There's

DID YOU KNOW

Henry Barber, the best and most innovative climber of the 70s, studied monkeys at Boston's Franklin Park Zoo. They taught him about body positions, momentum, straight-arm hangs, and the open grip. "Hot Henry" tore through the climbing world, smashing the status quo in many countries and leaving a legacy that will long be admired.

the *edging* hold: the inside edge of your climbing shoe is held firmly onto a sharp hold and your heel is elevated to increase edging power. Such a move works when the hold is sharp, square, and well-defined. If the hold is ill-defined or sloping, you'll get better purchase lowering your heel and putting more rubber to the rock. Lowering the heel also reduces the dreaded foot wobble that results from both fear and weak feet. The strongest use of your foot will be on its inside edge. The outside edge is also useful (and underused by most climbers) both as a powerful way to use your foot and a fundamental method of extending your reach. Using the outside edge requires shifting your body to the side and pulling sideways onto a hold in a kind of modified layback maneuver (see page 40).

Front-pointing, using the front end of the shoe alone, is generally not very effective: The climbing shoe is too flexible and your big toe isn't as strong as the sides of your foot. In some kinds of rock — pocketed limestone, for example — such front-pointing may be useful, but it won't be part of your standard repertoire as you begin.

SMEARING When the footholds are rounded or sloping downward, the edging hold doesn't work. Too little rubber is applied to the rock, and the edge of the shoe skates off the hold. Rounded or sloping holds need to be *smeared* or used with maximum rubber contact to the rock surface. Such a *friction hold* sometimes requires dropping the heel or bending the underfoot so that you can put as much surface area down as possible. Remember that the rock is coarse and crystalline and that you want to get as much as you can of this "sandpaper" surface to stick into the soft rubber of your soles. Place your foot deliberately, imagining the jagged little points of rock digging into your sole. Make sure no grit or gravel is underfoot (whenever you hear that gritty noise of sand underfoot, you can clean the shoe by simply wiping it against your other leg; long pants are helpful for this one).

Wiggle your heel just a bit after placing your foot on a friction hold. This will help you "set" your foot and also ascertain its security. Once you decide that you are going to use a particular foothold, use it with confidence. If instead you still have a nagging doubt, you'll use the foot more tentatively, unconsciously unweighting it from its purchase and increasing the chance that it will slip. LOOK AT YOUR FEET Edging and smearing require attention to the rough surface on which you are climbing. Keep your eyes down, checking carefully for any scoops or depressions, tiny knobs, crystals, or even rough spots on the wall. No foot should ever be placed without your deliberate intention, and no foot should ever be placed without your watching it land surely on the exact spot you have chosen. Beginners typically look desperately upwards, hoping to find the hand-hold that will save them. Experienced climbers keep their eyes on their feet, knowing that the subtle work here makes the difference between efficient climbing and failure.

The wear pattern of a climber's shoes tells quite a bit about his technique. If the toe alone is bearing the brunt of the wear, the climber has probably not been creative enough in his foot placements. And if the toe of the shoe is wearing out right where the sole meets the upper rubber "rand," then he must be sloppily dragging his foot as he moves upward. This is not only inefficient, but costly in shoe

"Flagging" with his left foot, this climber demonstrates one of the many ways to keep the body in balance even on the most difficult terrain.

repair. Look for a wear pattern that is spread about the front of the sole, not limited to the big-toe area. This suggests that you are taking advantage of the many ways the shoe can be used on a variety of holds.

Finally, you won't know the limits of your footwork until you push it to failure. On a safe top-rope, you can experiment and learn that fine line between a foot that will hold and one that won't.

Your Body

Your hands and feet don't do all the climbing. Be ready to call the rest of your body into service when the need arises. Shoulders can provide balance as you lean into an inside corner. Knees can stabilize you as to seek a clever rest. Elbows splayed out against the rock, outrigger fashion, make fine stabilizers as you adjust your feet and bring your body into a position of balance. Although there are some distinct principles involving the uses of hands and feet, the ingenious uses of your entire body are too numerous to catalog. Your challenge is to discover them.

Solid hand jams and lots of air below.

GEARING UP FOR THE NEWCOMER

Y̲ou just bought your first snowboard and you're still paying off that new kayak, so you're wondering what all of this climbing gear is going to cost. Not much, actually. Although there are a lot of impressive gadgets out there — fancy quick-clipping carabiners, exotic spring-loaded anchors, and countless other gizmos that can efficiently separate you from your money — in the beginning, you should keep it simple. Hold off buying the high-tech gear until you know what to do with it.

The rope has always been the symbol of the sport, but it won't be your first purchase. Gyms provide their own ropes, and since you'll be going out with more experienced climbers as you begin outdoors, they will bring the rope and anchoring hardware.

Your needs are far simpler. They are:

Climbing shoes	$130
Harness	$60
Locking carabiner	$15
Belay/rappel device	$15
Helmet (especially if you plan to climb outdoors)	$60
Chalk bag (some might disagree here)	$15

This starter package costs around $300. Gyms and guide services pro-

Getting to know the harness and basic tie-in method (page 81) will be your first step toward becoming familiar with climbing's specialized gear.

sole rubber can be laid down to maximize adhesion to the rock surface. On steep, horizontally-banded sandstone or on sharp, flaking granite, it demands being stiff enough to allow standing on a sharp half-inch foothold. On overhanging, pocketed limestone, it demands being so thin and malleable that your toes can actually grab the hold, much like another set of fingers. And, most demanding of all, certain conditions require that climbing shoes be mercilessly stuffed into cracks to gain purchase on the rock.

In short, no one shoe does it all. In varied climbing environments, a general use shoe serves nicely. Top climbers, of course, will tell you that it's not the shoe, it's the climber, and they'll be happy to drive the point home by waltzing up that route you've struggled on all day barefoot or in tennis shoes.

vide or rent basic gear, and many cautious shoppers wait until they have a better understanding of the sport before they invest in anything.

SHOES

Hiking shoes hike. Running shoes run. Climbing shoes climb, but it's not as simple as that. Climbing demands many things of a shoe. On low-angled smooth granite, it demands being so flexible that lots of

Today's Climbing Shoes

The traditional mountain boot was an ankle-high, stiff, leather boot with a lugged rubber sole. It performed well over boulders, gripped its way on hard snow, kept the toes warm in the high mountains, and was stiff enough to be fitted with *crampons*, the ice-climber's spikes.

In the late 1960s, light-weight versions of the cleated mountain boot evolved: the first prototypes of the specialized rock climbing shoe. The biggest change since those early years was the disappearance of the cleats. Why were the soles cleated in the first place? To grip soft surfaces like mud or snow. Keep this in mind as you consider the reasoning behind today's smooth soles. It's impossible to bite into hard rock. Instead, the rock digs into the surface of the sole, and the more area of contact, the better the grip. A cleated sole has less surface area in contact with the rock. I tell my beginners to visualize a rock surface from an ant's perspective: The rock is rough and jagged, with huge pointed crystals biting into the rubber of the shoe. Keep this image in mind as you learn more about footwork.

Today's rock climbing shoes aren't called on to keep your feet warm or to hold crampons. The shoes

Mammut's Blast, a comfortable shoe for long routes and cracks, is relatively stiff for edging performance and offers enough support to prevent fatigue on big days.

you'll see at the gym or on the crag are soft, usually low-cut, smooth-soled, and very snug, more like a ballet slipper or a wrestling shoe than the mountain boots of alpine lore.

Types of Shoes

GENERAL PURPOSE Any shoe that doesn't profess to perform a specialty: it ought to be stiff enough to *edge*, yet flexible enough to *friction*. Edging is the technique of using the stiff side of the boot sole to stand on the tiny platform offered by a thin ledge or foothold, sometimes as narrow as an eighth of an inch. Conversely, frictioning means putting the whole flat forefoot onto the rock, as if you were trying to walk up a steep roof — the more contact area, the better the friction properties. Don't presume that "general purpose" means beginner or inferior. It refers to a good introductory shoe that will allow you to experiment with a variety of techniques and rock types. In fact, the best rock climbers refer to such a shoe as a "long route" shoe, meaning that it will meet all their needs and remain comfortable all day. Some of the specialized, super-tight shoes do nasty things to your feet in only a few hours. A general-purpose shoe may be either ankle high or cut low; the low cut allows greater ankle movement, though if you are climbing in wide cracks — Yosemite, for example — the ankle-high shoe offers better ankle protection. Yet don't expect any shoe to support your ankle like a high-top hiking boot. And don't do much walking in your climbing shoes; approach the

---

DID YOU KNOW

A revolution in climbing shoes began in the early 1980s when Spanish rubber arrived. The new shoes, called Fires (pronounced "fee-rays"), had soles so "sticky" that once-impossible friction moves became the norm, and climbers who used them thought that somehow they had woken up one morning and improved their skills a full grade. Other brands joined the revolution, and now all good shoes have rubber at least as useful as the 1983 imports.

---

cliffs in walking shoes and reserve the specialized footwear for the climb itself.

EDGING SHOES The stiff soles of these shoes allow you to stand more easily on sharp edges, sometimes little more than the thickness of a coin pasted onto the wall. A newcomer lacks the foot strength of a pro and sometimes finds the stiffer shoe to be helpful. A stiff shoe, however, limits foot movements. Climbing requires all sorts of creative foot positions, and it is difficult to conform a hard-edged climbing shoe to a sloped or rounded foothold.

Edging shoes are built either by incorporating some kind of stiffener into the sole (and drastically reducing sensitivity) or by being so tight that the foot itself provides the edging power. The latter shoe isn't very strong, however, if it's on a limp and untrained foot.

FRICTION SHOES Adhesion to a rock surface is achieved mainly from the area of rubber surface placed on the rock (and from the ant's viewpoint, the number of jagged crystals poking into that rubber). Friction shoes bend well underfoot allowing the larger part of the forefoot to be laid down flat on the rock. This is called *smearing*, a term that describes the compression of a lot of sole rubber onto a sloping hold to maximize adhesion. Edging shoes are too stiff to perform well in this department; their rigidity resists the deformation required of a good friction shoe.

An easy-on/easy-off slipper for bouldering, indoor use, and sport climbing.

When the wall you're climbing, indoors or out, overhangs, your feet become hands. The softer the shoe, the better it grabs. There are countless examples of difficult routes that, in the days before the specialization of rock shoes, were accomplished barefoot because that was the only way climbers could grab the holds on the overhanging wall.

New-age sport routes and indoor gym routes all seem to be of this overhanging genre. If you plan to climb predominantly indoors, consider friction shoes, even if you are a beginner. Remember, however, that your feet are more accustomed to walking and running and that toe strength will take time to acquire. SLIPPERS The least substantial climbing shoes, slippers are also called training shoes because they force your feet to exercise more strenuously. They don't have laces; instead, an elasticized top holds the foot in place. Slippers are particularly popular on overhanging gym or sport routes, where they give one the "feel" of climbing barefoot without the pain. Slippers aren't, however, practical for a beginner, especially one who plans to subject them to the rigors of real rock.

Fit

The standard sales pitch once went like this: "OK, now push your foot into the shoe. Come on. Harder. Go ahead, stamp it down. Now, how does that feel? It's killing you? Perfect."

?

DID YOU KNOW

American shoe company Five.Ten makes a sole compound called Stealth with a formula so jealously guarded that they won't even patent it, for fear of the secret getting out. When asked about the formula, Dr. Stealth says, "I could tell you, but then I'd have to kill you."

Fortunately, with the growth of the sport competition came to the shoe industry, and it didn't take manufacturers long to realize that a comfortable shoe would make happier feet and sell more shoes.

The ideal shoe fits a bare foot snugly enough so that there is no sloppy "dead" space, but not so tightly as to make your eyeballs bulge every time you put them on. The perfect fit will feel as if you've put your feet into wet clay or into a loose shoe that has had the air sucked out of it. It will feel as if the shoe was made for your foot.

Different companies build their shoes on different lasts, or patterns, and once you get to know some of the brands, you'll be able to predict what fits best for you. Some lasts are wider, some "boxier," some more pointed. It pays to shop around and try on as many brands as you can. A friend of mine in the gear business tells his customers not to shop for a brand or model of shoe but to find the one that fits.

Is there a rule of thumb (or toe) that guides shoe sizing? I put on a pair of shoes in the store over bare feet and walk around, browsing the other gear that I won't be able to afford that day. If after 15 minutes, the pain is unbearable, the shoe's too tight. If it seems that I could probably walk a half-mile without bleeding, then I'm close. If I could imagine comfortably walking two miles, then the shoe is too big. It takes experience to get it right. Just don't fall for the myth that you have to be in pain to climb well.

Cost

Keep in mind that a newcomer's sloppy footwork is rough on shoes, so your first pair isn't worth a huge investment. This is especially true outdoors; indoor walls are a little more forgiving. General-purpose shoes start at about $100, though as models change and as stores need to turn over their stock, you might find some sales. Top-end shoes are around $150. Rentals are available at some gear stores.

Upkeep

Wear climbing shoes *only* when climbing. Walk to the gym or local cliff wearing walking shoes or hiking

GEAR TALK

LEATHER STRETCH

Shoes with a fabric lining won't stretch very much. Unlined shoes, built of a single layer of leather, will stretch at least a full size. Buy unlined shoes tight and bear with them as they stretch to accommodate your foot.

boots. Even so, the rigors of climbing take their toll. A well-made shoe can be resoled several times at around $40 per job. It's time to resole when the rubber sole has almost worn through to the rand, the thin rubber strip, that wraps around the side of the shoe. Rand replacement is possible, but you'd be better off getting the job done before that is necessary.

Don't ask your local cobbler to work on your climbing shoes. Look instead in the climbing magazines for repair shops, costs, and mailing procedures (see Sources & Resources, page 183) or inquire at your local outfitter.

HARNESS

When my friend Bill encouraged me to tie in by simply wrapping the rope around my waist and securing it with a bowline, it made sense because I didn't know any better. In fact, over my first few years of climbing, I took several good long falls on the waist tie-in. Maybe my gut muscles were stronger then; maybe I just viewed the pain as climbing's incentive to not fall. Whatever the case, what made sense to me 20 years ago seems ridiculous now.

Climbing harnesses have evolved to become as comfortable as they are safe. A typical harness is made of wide nylon webbing — padded in sensitive areas — and is fastened around the waist by a metal buckle. Whatever its design, the harness is

really a separate waist belt with leg loops. I mention this because it's the waist belt that ultimately holds you in. The leg loops simply transfer some of the load to your butt instead of strangling you around the middle. Keep this distinction in mind. There will be times when you'll be linking things (carabiners and slings) to your harness, and when you do, they must be fully attached to the *waist belt* portion of the harness. Clip gear to the other pieces of the harness and you might be in for a letdown.

DIAPER STYLE Two harness designs are in common use. One is a waist belt with a diaperlike leg loop that pulls in from between the legs and is held in place by plastic clips. This style is preferred by guide services (because it is so adjustable), winter climbers (same reason), and women (you can drop the leg loops and thus your pants without unbuckling the harness). The only drawback is the omission of a belay loop, a handy feature that is integrated into the second common design.

LEG-LOOP STYLE This harness is the most common in use today. It's built of a waistband with leg loops attached below. The unit is held together by a *belay loop,* a super-tough webbing loop that serves as the attachment for belay and rappel devices. Don't tie your climbing rope to this loop; the rope ties directly through both the waistband and the leg loops. All harnesses come with instructions about fitting and tying-in: follow them exactly.

Fit

Some harnesses are adjustable — helpful for group work, when you're wearing varying layers of clothing, or whenever you break your diet. Notice that some harnesses have adjustable leg loops, an excellent idea so long as the buckles are positioned so that they don't grind into your flesh when you fall.

The *rise* of a harness is the distance between the waistband and the leg loops. On some harnesses the rise is adjustable. Women's harnesses are different mainly in the length of the rise and in the size of leg loops relative to waist belt.

Ask to hang in a harness before you buy it. It should be somewhat comfortable, transferring most of the load to your rear end and upper thighs without the waist belt riding up onto your ribcage. The waist belt should adjust snugly enough so that

Top: Most harnesses are constructed of a waist belt and set of leg loops held together by a stout belay loop. Bottom: This diaper-type harness allows the leg loops to drop free when nature calls, but it lacks the useful belay loop.

it's above your hip-bones, eliminating any chance of your falling out. If you fall upside-down, it's only your pelvis width that keeps the harness on, so check this fit carefully. Don't wear your harness low like a gunfighter's belt or a snow-boarder's pants. Keep it above your pelvic bone.

THE BUCKLE
You should have at least three inches of excess webbing after fastening the buckle and passing it back through to secure it. Most harnesses aren't secure until this double-pass has been done. Read carefully the directions for fastening your harness before using it.

Options

VELCRO CLOSURE Some harnesses have Velcro closures so that the harness stays snug while you cinch its buckle tight. I hope by now that you are skeptical enough to see the problem: Someone could just slap the Velcro on, intending to buckle the harness later, forget, and lose the whole thing. In a recent — and sensible — trend most companies have eliminated these "time-saving" features.

GEAR LOOPS These stiff loops on the waistband are very helpful for holding gear, especially for a lead climber. (They are clearly not built for load-bearing, but I have seen on two occasions people use them for such, one as part of an anchor tie-in and another beginner actually belaying from a loop!)

DOUBLEBACK SYSTEM This is a new and innovative buckle design from Petzl that remains threaded at all times. You step into the harness and cinch it up. It's impossible to forget to re-thread the buckle because it's already fixed in that position. Expect other companies to follow suit.

ONE-SIZE-FITS-ALL Some harnesses (Misty Mountain Fudge and the Blue Water Voyager, to name two) are fully adjustable and built from a single piece of webbing. They've become popular with S.W.A.T. teams and other groups of part-time climbers. The design is clever and useful, but the leg loops must be well-adjusted; if

For children, a full-body harness is required; kids don't have wide enough hips to securely hold an adult harness in place.

there's slack here, it could transfer to, and loosen, the waist belt in the event of a hard force.

CHEST HARNESS It used to be mandatory to wear a chest harness to keep upright in a fall. In fact, most manufacturers covered themselves from liability by printing a warning on harness tags that the rig "must be worn with a chest harness."

Few climbers actually did so, but at least the industry could say, "We told them to." Recent studies done by Union Internationale des Associations d'Alpinisme (UIAA), however, show that a chest harness could increase whiplash in the climber's neck in the event of a fall, and so UIAA's latest conclusion is that the chest harness might do more harm than good. Remember, though, that if the bones of your pelvis are not wider than the waist-belt circumference, then you need a chest harness as the only sure way to keep the harness on. This is the case with children and people with large bellies (or to be perhaps more sensitive, people of girth).

CHILDREN'S HARNESSES There are a few full-body harnesses that are built just for kids. The narrow pelvis structure of a child won't allow a waist belt to hold securely, and these new harnesses are excellent and safe.

Follow directions carefully for rigging.

Expect a harness to last a few years — less if you are aggressive (chimneying or shuffling around on your butt), but no more than five years, even if you use it sparingly. Many harnesses use a different color thread on seams to help you inspect for wear. Treat your harness the way you treat all nylon products: store it out of direct sunlight, keep it free from acids (batteries).

CARABINERS

You've seen *carabiners* dangling from backpacks and holding keys from belt loops. They have become a symbol of the sport, and as climbing becomes more fashionable, aspiring climbers use the carabiner to announce themselves as members of the chosen few. To start, you'll need just one locking carabiner to use with your belay device, but as you get into the sport, you'll be adding many more to your rack.

Three carabiners: A wide-mouth "HMS" locking 'biner (top) is most useful for belaying and rappelling. The basic "D" carabiner (middle) is simple and strong. While the oval (bottom) is beefy and heavy, its symmetry allows some inventive uses. It's the workhorse 'biner for the top-roper.

Locking vs. Non-Locking

For the most essential uses — belaying and rappelling — a locking carabiner is a must. Quite simply, it's less likely to open up unexpectedly. A hollow collar screws up over the gate, locking it in place. A locking carabiner might look beefy, but it is no stronger than another similar 'biner. It simply stays closed more reliably. Remember: It's only a locking carabiner if you remember to lock it!

Why not use locking carabiners exclusively? For top-roping, that's not a bad idea. But for lead climbing, where weight is an issue and, even more significant, where clipping in and out must often be done desperately with one hand, the locking carabiner isn't practical. You'll want a locking carabiner on your belay and rappel device, but remember that even a locking carabiner can be improperly loaded, putting stress on the weakest part, the gate. And even a locking carabiner can open accidentally if vibrations or rubbing against the rock cause the screw collar to rotate.

Shapes

The original, basic carabiner shape is the oval. One advantage is its simple construction and resulting lower cost. Another plus is that when two such ovals are doubled with the gates on opposite sides for security, the profile of the doubled carabiners is cleaner. You'll see this benefit when setting up top-ropes (see page 75).

The D-shaped 'biner is stronger. Look how it loads: The weight is applied inside the "elbow" of the carabiner, so the force is pulling straight in line with the strong shaft of the unit. Examine how an oval 'biner is loaded. The weight tries to unbend the carabiner, since the load isn't directly lined up with the strong shaft. (Think about how you would break a stick. Would you try to bend it till it broke, or would you simply try to pull it apart the long way?)

I'll discuss other more specialized carabiners in succeeding chapters as their special advantages come into play. These two shapes are adequate for your early climbs.

BELAY / RAPPEL DEVICE

The newcomer to climbing first needs to be a competent *belayer*. To *belay* means to tend the safety rope while your partner climbs, paying it out or taking it in, always ready to lock it off in the event of a fall. (Chapter 5, "Top-Roping," shows how to apply the technique you'll learn here.)

Simply put, any belay or rappel device adds friction to a rope to slow it down or lock it off. The most common is known as a *belay plate*. Older climbers might refer to it as a Sticht Plate, a specific early model. A loop of rope is squeezed through the plate and clipped into the locking carabiner. If fed smoothly, the rope runs without interference. When the "brake" side of the rope is pulled back, the rope pulls the plate hard toward the carabiner, and the rope is locked off. (I've heard of climbers using a single chain link for this purpose. Though I don't recommend this, it demonstrates how

The HB Sheriff (above) is one of several tube-type belay/rappel devices. It's simple, light, and versatile. Some traditional belay plates (right) have a spring that makes belaying easier for beginners by keeping the rope from jamming as it's fed.

simple the unit is.)

Most belay plates have twin holes for double-rope technique and doubled-rope rappelling. Use either hole singly for belaying.

A good variation on the flat plate belay device is the elongated tube type, with brand-names such as the Tuber from Lowe, the Pyramid from Trango, the Air Brake from Blue Water, the Air Traffic Controller from Black Diamond, and the Sheriff from HB.

Some climbers use a figure-8 descender for rappelling (and even belaying). It is the most traditional design, time-tested and simple. It's a bit heavier, however, than the tube-type unit, and its belay application is slightly inferior. Some "8s" have a small ring end designed to function like a flat belay plate (see page 82). Don't use the unit in its rappel mode for belaying; it is hard to feed quickly and it can't be locked off tightly in the event of a severe fall. Also avoid "sport belays." They are too loose to hold a heavy force.

The GriGri

The GriGri is a new device that locks off the rope when it is jerked with a mechanism much like that in a seatbelt. It's a fairly complicated device, and though it is becoming the norm in gyms, I don't recommend it as your first belay gadget. Learn the basic belay plate process, and you'll have a better understanding of the GriGri if you later choose to go that route. More on the GriGri in chapter 5.

HELMETS

A helmet can save you from death or brain injury. The beautiful people in the magazines, hair blowing in the breeze, don't look so glamorous on the ground with a head injury. Almost all other adventure athletes wear helmets; look for climbers to get on board as they come to realize that their most valued piece of gear sits on their shoulders. My snide answer to the newcomer who poses the question, "Will I need a helmet?" is, "If you ask

GEAR TALK

LOOK FOR THE UNION LABEL

The UIAA (Union Internationale des Associations d'Alpinisme) is the most widely respected agency in the establishment of safety standards, and any gear that carries the UIAA label can be considered safe. Some items — shoes, for example — don't really pose safety issues, so don't look for labeling on them. But on helmets and ropes and many brands of carabiners, look for the little UIAA tag before you set your money down.

You'll find a variety of helmets, made from either plastic or fiberglass. Whatever its construction, you must adjust it for a snug, secure fit. A head lamp (below) is easily attached if you find yourself out after dark.

the question, you probably don't." Unfortunately, even though it is dangerous to go bareheaded, most climbers still do, and so even for this book, there is a remarkable shortage of photographs depicting helmeted climbers. I wish we had more. Few indoor establishments currently require helmets. Their reasoning? The walls are so steep that falls are free-swinging and there is little chance of being hit by objects falling from above.

Helmets used to be heavy and cumbersome; no longer. They are lightweight, comfortable units that you won't even notice on your head. Two types of helmet suspension systems are available. The classic webbing harness that holds the shell away from your head is still the most common. Gaining favor, however, is a crushable foam liner that sits inside the hard shell, much like a bike helmet's. A bike helmet alone is insufficient. It protects against impact as it bangs against a road surface, but a falling rock would penetrate it, doing damage directly or catching the helmet and jerking it to the side injuring the neck. All climbing helmets must have a hardened shell for these reasons.

Your helmet must stay in place to be useful. Make sure that you wear yours just over your eyebrows. Some beginners think helmets are skull caps and wear them too far to the backs of their heads. Not too useful if the climber above kicks off a stone. As you fit a helmet, also consider whether you will need it in the winter; very few helmets are large enough to accommodate a winter hat.

Weights vary, and generally, the lighter, the weaker. The range is from about 11 ounces to 20 ounces. Some

CHALK AND CHALK BAGS

Most climbers use chalk, much like a gymnast, to keep their hands dry while climbing. The chalk doesn't help you to grip; it simply counters the sweat that oozes from your fingertips. Since it leaves a mark on the rock, it is controversial. Be responsible and don't make an unnecessary mess. Some routes, especially where it seldom rains (in dry climates or under overhangs) can be seen from a half mile away from the white chalk dots on the wall. Chalk also takes some of the mystery away. Climbers can simply stab for the white spots where others have gone before instead of having to figure things out for themselves.

There are a variety of chalk bags out there, though the choice isn't as crucial as that of other gear. Bags cost about $15, and are hung from a thin cord or belt tied around your waist. Make sure yours has a good closure; otherwise you'll lose chalk into your pack, making quite a mess.

There are a few ways to cut down on chalk's messiness. Colored chalk can be used to match the rock tone and reduce the visual impact. There are also some products — Grrrip, for example — that dry the fingers without leaving visible marks. You might also choose a fine mesh sack of chalk rather than keeping loose powder in the chalk bag; one such product is called a Bison Ball. Alternatively, you can fill and tie off the foot of a nylon stocking. Such sacks keep the chalk in place when a climber falls or sits down. They are usually required in a gym.

are more adjustable than others, some have lower, cleaner profiles and thus allow a wider range of head movements in tight spaces, and some are snazzier with bright colors and wild graphics (give me basic white, thank you).

The UIAA runs helmets through a battery of tests, examining side impact (as in a fall), top impact (as from falling rock), and even shock absorption (as in the kind of top impact that would damage your cervical spine). They've got a dummy head (there were lots of candidates here) wired with sophisticated sensors that record the impacts when banged and knocked about. The tests are rigorous and so are the standards for the UIAA label.

A helmet isn't useful in your pack. Wear it any time you are near the base of the cliff, belaying from below, climbing, or are in any conceivable danger from falling objects. Why take it off at all? Make it seem a part of you and you won't notice it.

Two tricks for transport: Don't clip your helmet to your harness when down-climbing. It will only bang on rocks as you squat and crouch your way down through the boulders. And don't set it down upside-down. Its capacity to roll will surprise you.

THE ROPE

The rope is the symbol of the sport and the tether that keeps you safe.

No single piece of gear is so fundamental to climbing. It's worth knowing something about the history and technology of rope manufacture before you rely so fully on your thin nylon cord.

TWISTED Mountaineers during the 1800s carried natural-fiber ropes with them as they made their ascents, mainly to assist weaker partners up hard sections and to allow for creative descents. Such ropes clearly wouldn't hold a hard lead fall. World War II brought synthetic fibers into rope manufacture with du Pont's new material called Nylon, and for the first time climbers could begin to push their limits with some confidence that their ropes could withstand a fall. The early nylon ropes were laid ropes, constructed much like the old hemp lines, bundled and twisted. These twisted ropes were strong, but they stretched too much. The falls could be held and the shock absorbed, but the rope would stretch as much as 40 percent, adding to the

DID YOU KNOW

Climbers can thank World War II for the technology that led to nylon, but they'd be surprised to learn that the first commerical use of nylon wasn't for rope. It was for the toothbrush.

dangers of hitting a ledge on the way down. Additionally, the twisted construction was tough to handle and often left the dangling climber spinning in air as the rope straightened under the load. The most common rope of this era and construction was called Goldline.

KERN-MANTLE In the 1950s, a new type of construction was offered to climbers. It consisted of a core of fibers covered and protected by a woven sheath. This core-sheath construction is called *kern-mantle*, and soon it became the standard. Its advantages are many: It handles much more easily, twists much less, absorbs shock-loading without as much stretching, and best of all, it keeps its load-bearing elements protected inside the sheath. When a laid rope becomes fuzzy with use, every single strand might be cut, since at regular intervals each strand rises to the surface of the twisted bundles. In the case of kern-mantle rope, the wear that occurs on the sheath is unrelated to the real strength of the rope hidden in the internal core.

Ropes today come in a wide variety of lengths, thicknesses, and colors, but they are essentially no different from those revolutionary ones

of 40 years ago. Climbers generally use ropes of either 165 or 200 feet (50 to 60 meters) in length with diameters ranging from 11mm for heavy-use top roping to 9.5 mm where weight is a factor. Your first rope should be a beefy 10.5 mm or 11 mm one that will wear better than a thinner one, an important lconsideration when subjecting the rope to the abrasion of top-roping and lowering.

Ropes with a water-resistant coating are also available, adding a few dollars to the price tag. The new "dry" ropes do absorb much less water and are preferred by ice-climbers and alpinists, yet worn dry rope absorbs water much like an uncoated one. There are numerous water-repellent rope technologies on the market, but none has truly succeeded in keeping ropes dry during a rain.

Care of Rope

Keep your rope out of direct sunlight when not in use. Ultra Violet (UV) radiation degrades nylon, and while normal use isn't a problem, don't store your

Indian Creek Canyon, southeast Utah. Once equipped and skilled, you'll focus not on the gear but on the magical heights to which it can bring you.

rope in a window or leave it hanging out in sunlight for extended periods. Don't step on your rope. When the rope has gotten dirty, tiny crystals will abrade the fibers from within. Wash your dirty rope in a bathtub of either plain water or a very gentle detergent like Woolite, and let it drip

GEAR TALK

DON'T ASSUME YOUR ROPE IS LONG ENOUGH

If you are sport-climbing and lowering from fixed anchors, make sure that the free end of the rope is tied either to the belayer or to an anchor on the ground. The anchors might be more than a half-rope length away, and the free end of the rope could slip through the belay if the rope isn't secured. This is entirely preventable, yet it is happening with increasing frequency.

dry. You'll be surprised how much sand is left in the tub after a washing. *Do this by hand.* Don't subject your best friend to the uncertainties of a mechanical washing machine or the heat of a dryer.

Expect a rope to last couple of seasons of occasional use, though the rope's actual lifetime depends a great deal on the coarseness of the rock you climb, your care when setting up anchors, the number of rappels and lowerings, and the other abuses you might inflict on it. When to retire a rope?

● When the sheath is so fuzzy (half the sheath fibers are severed) that you just don't feel comfortable with it.

GALILEO AND NEWTONS

In the late 1500s, standing from a railing atop the Leaning Tower of Pisa, Galileo demonstrated that gravity increases the velocity of all falling objects to the same degree, regardless of their relative weights. Now aren't you reassured to know that even the skinniest elite sport climber will be subjected to the same plummet as the beefiest weekend warrior? Fall the full length of a climbing rope — the worst case imaginable — and you will be traveling almost 70 miles an hour. And as the worn-out joke goes, it's not the fall that will get you, it's the sudden stop.

To begin our discussion of how the climbing rope and belay methods lessen the suddenness of the stop, picture this: Would you rather run into a brick wall or a mattress? You chose the mattress (I hope) because it is softer. Actu-ally, you chose it because it brings you to a stop less abruptly.

So it is with a climbing fall. If your rope were to bring you to an abrupt halt from your 50 or 70 miles-an-hour velocity, you'd be killed by the stop. Your bones just couldn't take the pressures. Research done for the military concerning impacts as parachutes opened concluded that a healthy human body can withstand a maximum impact somewhere around 12 kiloNewtons of force — around 2,700 pounds. This research was instrumental to UIAA as it designed standards for ropes.

The KiloNewton
The impacts and strengths you'll encounter in the climbing world are measured using the metric system. A kilogram is equal to approximately 2.2 pounds. A Newton is the unit of force required to move one kilogram one meter per second per second.

❷ If the white core fibers are visible at an abraded spot (though you might just cut it here and have a perfectly operable but shorter rope).

❸ After the rope has been subjected to a really hard lead fall. Remember, it's not necessarily the length of the fall that counts as much as the ratio between the length of the fall and the amount of rope out to absorb the impact.

❹ After five years. An old rope shouldn't be used for leading. This applies even to an unused rope that has been kept in careful storage; it's shock-absorption capacity diminishes over time regardless.

❺ After seven years. Such a rope

Climbing gear is generally rated in kiloNewtons (kN) since it doesn't really hold a static weight, but instead changes the inertia of a mass. One kiloNewton, then, is a force of approximately 220 pounds. A carabiner rated to, say, 24 kN will resist a force of over 5,000 pounds.

Dynamic climbing ropes (as opposed to *static* ropes, specifically built to have low stretch) must be able to reduce the impact on the climber, the belayer, and the protection by arresting the fall over a period of time.

To earn a UIAA label, a dynamic rope must demonstrate that it can successfully bring forces in a fall below the maximum of about 2,700 pounds. Remember, if the rope didn't absorb much of this force, then the stress on the system could well exceed the breaking strengths of all of the gear involved. The rope's cushioning effect, then, is essential to the safety system.

Sample strands of rope are tested by subjecting them to worst-case falls. The UIAA test uses an 80 kG weight attached to a three-meter length of rope. The weight is dropped over a 10-mm edge to simulate a carabiner. This "carabiner" edge is just above the anchor, making the total length of fall five meters. The "impact force" of the first of a series of falls must not exceed 1,200 kG (approximately 2,700 pounds). Subsequent falls result in higher and higher impact-force figures as the rope loses its capacity to absorb shock. Most ropes can absorb between five and ten such falls before finally breaking. Because the test itself damages the rope, the rope you buy will not have been tested. Samples from the manufacturer will instead have been used as standards.

shouldn't even be used for top-roping.

● If the rope has been exposed to acid. Storing your rope in a closed car trunk along with a spare automobile battery can seriously degrade the rope without showing any visible signs of damage.

Having said all this, I remind you that no dynamic rope has ever broken during use. There are countless examples of ropes being severed by abrasion or when running over a jagged rock edge during a fall, but ropes just don't break during regular use. Yes, you should treat your rope with the best of care and retire it if there is ANY doubt about its integrity. But the real dangers you face on the cliffs will come from the crystalline surface and jagged edges of rock.

T O P - R O P I N G

Although some guide services prefer to give their beginning clients an overview of the experience by taking them along on an easy multi-pitch climb, it's more likely that you'll begin on a *top-rope*. This means that you'll have a snug safety line covering you if you slip. The rope doesn't drag you up the cliff; it merely stays with you as you rely on hands and feet to move upward. Experienced climbers prefer a loose top-rope that will catch them in the event of a fall, but won't interfere with their climbing. A nervous beginner, however, usually likes the rope kept a bit tighter; that gentle tug from above is certainly reassuring.

Climbers choose a top-rope over lead-climbing for a number of reasons. It lets the beginner learn the sport without the uncertainty that goes along with leading, it provides good quick practice for seasoned climbers, and it allows the experts to push their physical limits knowing that they can do so without worry. Take a look at the history of the sport and you'll see how much relying on the rope has meant to progress. Former American Alpine Club President John Case, one of the country's pioneers of roped rock-climbing, never took a single fall in a climbing career that spanned more than 50 years. Top climbers today, on the

Indoors or out, the top-rope depends on solid and redundant anchors.

other hand, consider falling to be the requisite for progress. If you aren't willing to fall, they argue, you aren't willing to improve.

The most common top-rope system is referred to as a *slingshot* belay. A rope tied to a climber runs up to a secure anchor above, through a couple of carabiners which serve as pulleys, and back down to the ground

to an attentive *belayer*, the partner who keeps the rope snug as the climber moves up and who is ready at all times to lock off the rope should the climber fall. Once the climber reaches the anchor carabiners at the top, the belayer takes the climber's full weight and lowers her back down to the ground.

The process of top-rope belaying

is essentially the same whether you're in the gym or at a crag, with the one difference being in the anchors: gyms have top-ropes set up when you arrive; all you'll need are good belaying skills. Outside on real rock, you'll have to choose and set up your own top anchors. Indoors or out, the system is fairly simple, but you must understand and double-check each component. Remember: the law of gravity is strictly enforced.

A skilled and attentive belayer allows you to focus on the climb itself.

TOP ANCHORS

As you get into climbing, you'll probably be relying on anchors set up by experienced climbers; initially you'll have your hands full just learning sound belaying and basic climbing techniques. But since no top-roped climb could begin without such an anchor system established, we'll begin our discussion on the set-up as a whole before moving on to harness tie-ins and belay technique.

SECURE BACKUP SYSTEMS

Professional guides use the acronym R.E.N.E to describe their anchor systems. It stands for Redundant, Equalized, with No Extensions. This makes up what they call a "bombproof" anchor. *Redundancy* is the key. Never trust your life to one piece of gear. Sure, the label boasts of astronomical strengths, but a safe climber is a skeptical climber. I always set my anchors up not with the idea that individual elements might fail, but with the idea that they will fail. If this is your approach to setting up a system, you'll be especially careful to double everything in it. A huge tree is probably good by itself, but if there's any doubt at all, use more than one. Use separate slings, not just an extra-long one doubled. This is strong, but it's not redundant. And

continued on page 74

use opposite and opposed locking carabiners. Try an imaginary "cut test" on your anchors. Pretend that you have a pair of super bolt cutters and are allowed to snip any single part of your anchor. If any such cut would lead to total anchor failure, then the anchor wasn't redundant in the first place.

Equalization is a useful concept but not essential in most systems. It is a process by which the primary and the backup anchors share the load, thus cutting the stress in half. Ways to equalize the loads on slings are shown in chapter 6, "Leading," page 115.

The *No Extensions* part of the anchor is also vital. If your backup anchor has too much slack or if it is placed off too far to the side, then some pretty scary forces will build up on the secondary anchor if the primary anchor fails. Such forces could be large enough to break the secondary anchor as well, and then... Make sure that your backup anchor is snug with the primary anchor (six inches of slack is a maximum here). Then, if there's a failure to the first, the backup is employed quickly and effectively without shock-loading.

A good top-rope climb has a fairly straight line (to prevent a swinging fall), no loose rock or debris around the top that could be dislodged by the rope, and good hefty anchors near the edge. Seventy-five feet is about the maximum practical height, since most climbing ropes are around 165 feet long and the rope must run from the ground up through the anchors and back to the ground. Although there are endless kinds of anchors that can be combined to make a secure top point, the simplest and most reliable outdoor anchor is probably a large tree. We'll begin our discussion here.

Find a safe way around to the top of the cliff, and approach the edge carefully. It doesn't make much sense to risk your life just setting up the rope. If the edge is sloping or slippery, or if the situation seems in any way treacherous, secure yourself before you begin by clipping yourself in to a long sling hitched around a safe tree. Give a warning shout to let folks below know that you're up there and that the potential for falling objects exists. If, despite being extra careful, you still dislodge something, scream "Rock!" as loudly as you can, whether it's a boulder or just a stray carabiner. Everyone at the base of a cliff should be constantly on guard: with helmets on, out of the line of

Instead of tying your own webbing slings, you can buy pre-sewn "runners" of either nylon (left) or super-strong Spectra (right).

possible rockfall, or ready to scurry under some overhang or behind a large tree at the first shout from above.

Webbing anchors, like the slings shown on the trees on page 76, have long been a standard, mainly because the webbing material is strong (1-inch web holds about 4,000 pounds), inexpensive and readily available. One-inch nylon tubular webbing material can be bought at any climbing shop right off the spool. Beware, however, of any taped section on the webbing as it is rolled off the spool; it could hide the connection of a splice from the factory. I know of at least one case in which a climber failed to check under that mysterious piece of tape. The sling broke as soon as it was weighted!

There are two drawbacks to using webbing for top-rope anchors. First, the water knots (see page 121) used to secure them loosen over time; check them frequently. Second, it's tough to get the lengths between your primary and backup systems just right. Unless you are either patient or lucky, you will end up with too much slack in your backup sling, resulting in severe shock-loading if the primary anchor fails (see "Secure Backup Systems," page 73).

Author's Top-Rope Set Up

A good solution is to subsitute static rope for the webbing. (Eleven millimeter static rope is tough, but it doesn't stretch. For this reason it isn't used for climbing, but it's especially useful for anchoring and rappelling.) Slide a 4-foot length of tubular webbing onto the middle of a 50-foot length of static rope, creating a tough sheath covering the mid-section of the rope. Tie a figure-8 on a bight onto the sheathed section of rope. You now have a pre-tied top-roping tool that is safe, simple and quick to set up.

Now call "Rope!" loudly to warn those below that you are dropping a rope. Wait a moment to make sure that everyone has heard and responded to your call. Clip the center of the climbing rope to the loop of your static anchor rope (the figure-8 sheathed in webbing) via two locking, opposite-and-opposed locking carabiners, and then lower the two strands of the climbing rope over the cliff. Getting the ends to the ground can be frustrating if the rock is less than vertical or if there are trees or other obstructions along the way.

When you've got the anchor carabiners just over the edge, tie one end of the anchor rope to the tree farther from the edge, using a retraced

Typical Top-Rope Set Up

A typical top-rope anchor using webbing on trees. Slings are either tied around the tree (left tree), girth-hitched (right tree), or V-hitched (see below). Whatever the method of attachment, it's tough to get your lengths just right to equalize the load. For a clever alternative, see page 78.

To climber

To belayer

To belayer

To climber

figure-8 knot (it helps to step gently on the anchor rope to hold it in place while you are tying to the tree). Tying to the tree farther from the edge first gives you the advantage of being able

Slinging Trees

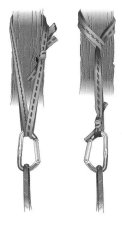

The V-hitch (left) is stronger, but unless the sling is long enough, the two strands in the carabiner could pull against each other and the load could fall back on the weak cara-biner gate. The girth hitch (right) is slightly weaker, but more secure because the weakness of the V-hitch is elimi-nated. Both are common set-ups.

to attach yourself to the anchor rope via a sliding prusik knot (see "Knots," page 119) clipped to your harness to keep you safe as you approach the edge and the second tree. Don't skip this step if the tree is dangerously close to the brink or on any kind of sloping and slippery ter-rain. If both trees are safely back from the edge, all the better.

Next, pull the remaining end of the static rope up just snug to the weight of the rope below and give a *tensionless wrap* around the second tree. This is not only very strong, but it's also the easiest way to adjust the length of the second leg of the static anchor rope. The two legs of the anchor are sharing the load, and your anchor carabiners are just over the edge of the cliff so that the climbing rope won't be subjected to the abra-sion of the cliff edge. This means that the climber "tops out" when reaching the carabiners, not by climbing up onto the ledge (which would increase the chance that the climber would dis-lodge rocks or dirt onto the belayer).

Look at your system now and give it the imaginary cut test. Two trees, two strands of rope, two carabiners, and even two load-bearing elements in the knotted loop — the rope itself and the webbing, which is both a sheath to protect the loop and a backup if the rope inside the knot were to fail.

USING FIXED ANCHORS

A 50-foot length of static rope, sheathed at the knot with 1-inch tubular nylon webbing, makes the quickest and most versatile top-anchor system.

In some areas, there simply aren't convenient or reliable trees for anchoring at the tops of the climbs. In most such areas, local climbers have installed fixed expansion-bolt anchors for top-rope use. (The term *fixed* refers to any devices deliberately left in place for future use.)

SLING ANGLES

When using more than one anchor, it's important not to have sling angles that are too wide. As you can see in the diagram, two parallel anchor slings essentially share the load, half on each. As the sling angle widens, so does the force on each. (Think about a suspension bridge or a ski lift; the droop in the cable is necessary to keep the line from breaking. The straighter the line, the more the forces accumulate.) Not only does a too-wide sling angle create huge forces, but it also means that the climber will take a nasty swing if one does fail. The swing will endanger the climber, severely abrade the remaining sling, and dislodge debris as it drags across the slope.

5° = 51 lbs. per anchor

90° = 70 lbs. per anchor

150° = 200 lbs. per anchor

100 lbs.

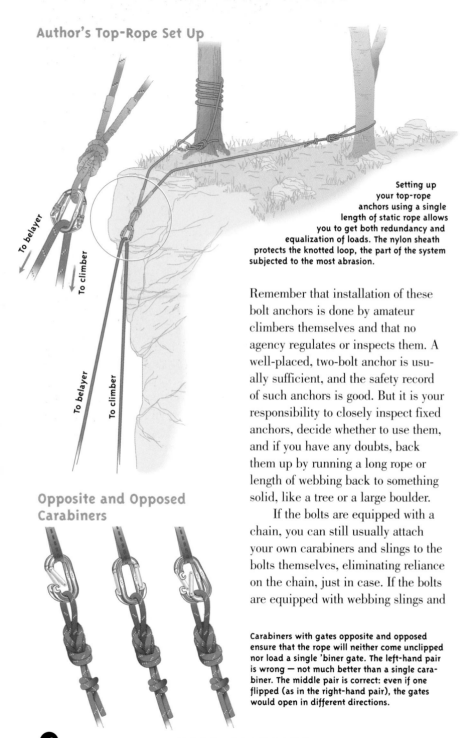

Author's Top-Rope Set Up

To belayer

To climber

To belayer

To climber

Setting up your top-rope anchors using a single length of static rope allows you to get both redundancy and equalization of loads. The nylon sheath protects the knotted loop, the part of the system subjected to the most abrasion.

Remember that installation of these bolt anchors is done by amateur climbers themselves and that no agency regulates or inspects them. A well-placed, two-bolt anchor is usually sufficient, and the safety record of such anchors is good. But it is your responsibility to closely inspect fixed anchors, decide whether to use them, and if you have any doubts, back them up by running a long rope or length of webbing back to something solid, like a tree or a large boulder.

If the bolts are equipped with a chain, you can still usually attach your own carabiners and slings to the bolts themselves, eliminating reliance on the chain, just in case. If the bolts are equipped with webbing slings and

Opposite and Opposed Carabiners

Carabiners with gates opposite and opposed ensure that the rope will neither come unclipped nor load a single 'biner gate. The left-hand pair is wrong — not much better than a single carabiner. The middle pair is correct: even if one flipped (as in the right-hand pair), the gates would open in different directions.

rings, be especially wary and back up the system with your own carabiners and slings attached to the bolts themselves.

However you set up your anchor station, make sure that the top rope is running through at least two solid anchor points and that the loading is nearly equalized between the two anchor points. Use the following checklist:

A busy top-rope area can become quite a social event. Just don't let the conversation distract you from your belaying duties.

❶ Never rely on one anchor point or carabiner in any top-rope set-up. Every element serving in the anchor system must have a backup.

❷ Use your own slings and carabiners as much as possible when using fixed anchors.

❸ Never run your rope directly over nylon slings. Nylon moving on nylon will surely melt the anchor sling.

❹ Never top-rope directly from rings or chains; a sandy rope will quickly wear out the fixed anchors.

BOTTOM ANCHORS

What? You're going to tie your belayer to the ground? Are you afraid she might run out for a cup of coffee? Actually, it's useful for a belayer on the ground to be tied securely to a bottom anchor. A falling climber can generate quite a bit of force, and a lightweight or inattentive belayer could be "swept off her feet," not by the sweet talk of her climbing partner, but because the big oaf blew a sequence and lobbed off the rock.

The bottom anchor isn't as crit-

Teaching the concept of the *brake hand*, fundamental to safe belaying.

ical as the top anchor (being supplemented naturally by the weight of the belayer herself). Most climbers use a single anchor point, one that needs to resist only moderate upward forces. Tying your belayer to the ground ensures that she'll stay put in the event of a fall, but it also prevents her from running if a loose rock is dislodged by the climber. It's crucial, therefore, for the belayer to be stationed in a safe place, far enough to the side or back from the rock so that there's no risk of her being clobbered from above.

You will see climbers, both in the gym and at the crags, belaying without tying themselves in. They can only do so if they are directly below the anchor. Otherwise, they run the risk of

being yanked over or pulled into the wall, losing control of the belay. As you start, take the more conservative approach and tie your belayer to the ground, either with the rope itself or by hitching the back of her harness to a tree or other ground anchor.

Belay Directly from the Anchor
Some people belay right off the stationary anchor on the ground. This removes the belayer as a backup and transfers the load directly to the anchor. The anchor-point strength and security are vital here, and all the rules of R.E.N.E. (see "Secure Backup Systems," page 73) apply. Note also that the belayer must be positioned close enough to such a static anchor to effectively break the force of the fall by properly employing his brake hand. Too far forward here and the braking is impossible. Warning: A static anchor is suitable only for a top-rope belay. It stops the fall so abruptly that the forces are increased on the anchors, acceptable in most top-roping situations but absolutely forbidden for a falling leader, who could be generating much more force on dubious protection. More on this in chapter 6, "Leading."

TYING IN TO THE HARNESS
The belay process won't do much good unless the climber is safely in the harness and the harness is tied onto the rope. Mistakes here have needlessly cost lives. Tie in with a

retraced figure-8 as shown (below). BOTH the belayer and the climber should inspect the harness and knot before any climbing takes place. Look to see that:

● the harness is snug and the buckle correctly fastened;

● the rope passes through the harness according to the manufacturer's instructions; and

● the knot is correct and backed up with a double overhand knot.

Make a habit of checking these three elements before your feet ever leave the ground.

BELAYING

Unless you are an airline pilot or a heart surgeon, never will you feel so directly responsible for the lives of others as when you are belaying. You, and you alone, have in your hands the safety of a climber high above who is counting on you to perform well. When you say, "On Belay," you are

Tying In To the Harness

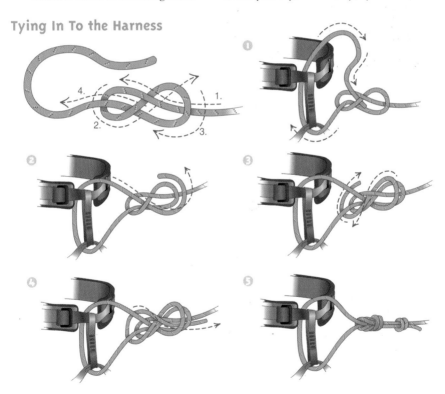

Tie-in method using a retraced figure-8 knot backed up with a double overhand knot. When tying in, always check to see that: 1) you've taken one last look at your buckle to make sure it is passed back through as designed, 2) the rope passes correctly through the harness, 3) the knot is correct and backed up. These three checks *must* be part of a life-long habit. And don't be shy about checking your partner as well.

Body Belay

Early climbers used the body, or hip, belay. While it's less secure than a good mechanical belay, experienced climbers keep it in their bag of tricks should they lose belay gear or find their ropes frozen too stiff to pass through a conventional belay device. The brake-hand sequence is the same (see page 83). Note the guide carabiner on the waist belt; it gives the belayer better control if the pull is off to the side.

The SBG belay plate, similar to HB Sheriff (page 61), also incorporates two sizes of braking grooves to provide extra braking power. For the ultimate in friction, it can be threaded as a hybrid figure-8 device for descending.

making a sacred pledge, one that you can only make when you are well-trained, well-practiced, and absolutely sure that you've got it right.

The process, while profoundly important, is simple. It involves managing the rope, taking rope in or paying it out depending on the direction in which the climber is moving, and locking it off securely in the event of a fall. Traditionally, climbers used a "body" or "hip" belay, wrapping the rope around their waist or under their buttocks to create enough friction to arrest a fall. This old-fashioned method isn't as secure as the newer, mechanical belays, but it's essential to know what to do if you lose your belay gadget and have to function gearless. Remember, however, that the traditional method is generally considered inferior to mechanical belaying and relatively useless if you plan to lower someone from high on a climb: it's hard to control and the seat of your pants just won't tolerate such extended friction.

Both belays work by adding friction to the rope. The traditional belay simply uses the friction of the body, while the mechanical belay uses the friction created by bending the rope radically around the locking carabiner. Both rely on one key hand to do the braking; this brake hand is fundamental, and it stays on the rope until your partner is safely on the ground. Period.

Holding a rope in braking position is easy: you simply pull back on

Hand Sequence for a Safe Belay

Follow this hand sequence closely and keep your brake hand on and ready at all times. 1 & 2) The brake, or right, hand is in position while the left pulls in rope to keep tight to the moving top-roped climber. 3 & 4) The guide, or left, hand is free to grab the brake rope *above* the brake hand. The guide hand holds the rope while the brake hand slides back into place. Keep the fingers of your brake hand closed around the rope throughout this sequence; a fall could occur at any second. 5) Once the brake hand is back in place, the sequence is ready to repeat. Feeding rope is easier than bringing it in. Just push out rope with your guide hand while your brake hand remains in ready position.

the brake hand and the rope will jam. The trouble comes when you try to take in rope without letting go of your brake hand. (Don't! Not even for a second while you switch hands!)

Follow the step-by-step sequence shown at right. The safest place to learn is on a flat surface, imagining that it is inclined. The "climber" can take some running "falls" and if the belayer goofs, the consequence will be nothing more than grass stains. If you are going to learn on the steep, it's essential that an experienced belayer hold the brake end of the belay rope as a safeguard so that even if you slip with your hand sequence, the second belayer is there to be your brake hand.

As you learn the procedure (and there are some variations here), expect to fumble. The dexterity required to be a good belayer takes time and repetition. It will — and it must — become second nature. Watch your hands, not the climber. Practice, practice, and practice. And

Proper lowering uses both hands as brakes. The lower one is used both as a backup and a way to get kinks out before they jam the system. Note that the belayer is firmly tied down and able to transfer the load to the anchor instead of being lifted off balance by the weight of the climber.

then when you are sure you've got it right, practice some more.

Some gyms and guides will show you a variation of this method that uses the fingers of the guide hand to pinch the brake side of the rope while the brake hand slides back into place. The method I describe is a little more secure because it doesn't require the finger coordination, and it can be used in winter while wearing gloves or even mittens.

Lowering is quite simple: Once the climber reaches the anchors, tighten up the belay and hold the rope in brake position (use two hands as shown) while the climber leans back on the rope. Only when you have received the full weight of the climber can you begin a slow and

steady lowering. Watch the braid of rope as it passes through your belay device in order to monitor the speed of the descent.

Belaying From the Top

The sling-shot belay described above is by far the most common top-rope belay. It's also possible, however, to belay from the top of the cliff. Such a top belay allows you to use the full length of the rope, expanding your options well beyond the seventy-five-foot half rope limit of the sling-shot method. It does, however, put much greater loads on the belayer, and so the top anchor must be secure and redundant. Allow for stretch in the anchor rope by sitting back from the edge (I learned the hard way by getting dragged right over the edge — I held on, but it was a close call). Remember, the top belayer must be well anchored and securely positioned because the load could be huge. That's why it's much better to set up the sling-shot whenever possible.

The GriGri

Petzl of France introduced a belaying product that is revolutionizing top-rope belaying and increasingly becoming the standard in gyms. It works much like an auto's seat belt locking mechanism. When the rope is fed out gently, the cam stays loose and the rope runs free. When the rope is jerked, as in a fall, the cam locks into position and the rope is

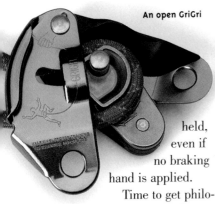

An open GriGri

hand-held wonder, knows its limitations, and can function without it. American educators are fretting about the future of the country if all of its students are skilled only at punching little buttons with no recollection of their multiplication tables.

held, even if no braking hand is applied.

Time to get philosophical. History is the story of mankind learning to apply technology to do jobs more efficiently. The cannon was better than the slingshot. The calculator beats the slide rule. But a good soldier knows hand-to-hand combat and a real engineer knows how to calculate, understands what's going on inside that little

And so it is with climbing's innovations, many of which you'll see in the rest of this book. Each does its job fairly well. Each was designed to make the sport safer and easier, yet in doing so, each took the place of some ingenuity that was formerly needed to do the same job. As you become a climber, challenge yourself to understand and be competent with the original methods. Not only will they help you understand the inner workings of the newest wonder-gadget

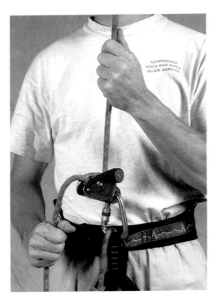

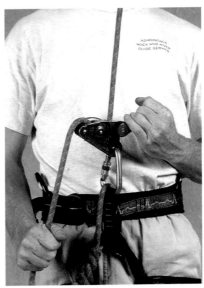

Left: Even though the GriGri is self-locking, you should still keep your brake hand on at all times. Right: The left hand holds the handle, unlocking the rope for lowering, while the right hand remains a ready brake hand.

of the day, but they'll also serve you well when some unanticipated circumstance requires you to get down to basics, drawing on your skills in the place of technology. And never pass up the opportunity to spend time with older climbers, the more experienced the better. Listen to their tales and watch them in action. They might dismiss the new ways with the old cliché, "We never used to..." Instead of tuning them out, you'd be wise to pay attention. Like the old fishermen or cowboys, they know tricks that will amaze you and that one day may save your life. In the grand continuum of resources that a good climber depends on, there's technology, then there's knowledge, but at the top is wisdom. Remember this and let it grow.

Now back to the GriGri. It's a wonderful little device, and it *almost* eliminates the human errors that can creep into belaying. In fact, many gyms require their use for top-rope climbing. (It's hard to feed rope smoothly to a lead climber, and a lead fall ought to have a "softer" belay to absorb some of the impact.) If your partner is inattentive or pulled off his feet, or even injured by a falling object, the camming mechanism will jam and the rope will be held fast. But remember, I said *almost*. The GriGri can be improperly loaded, or the release handle can be inadvertently held open, and if either occurs, then the unit won't hold.

There's also an insidious risk

associated with such gadgets: Climbers come to think that the piece no longer enhances the skill, but replaces it. Bad thinking indeed. And especially so if the climber ends up later using a belay method that doesn't incorporate the automatic locking mechanism of the GriGri. Such a climber may have established some sloppy belay habits with the automatic device, habits that will be disastrous when he is relying on the more traditional, low-tech gear.

The moral of this protracted story: your habits need to be sound, no matter how impressive the gear and no matter how many bells and whistles adorn it. In the case of the GriGri, keep a few things in mind. First, the brake hand stays on the rope at all times, just as with a traditional belay. Never hold the unit open as you pay out or take in rope. And as with every method, practice, practice, practice. The fancy new gear is no excuse for not having fully-honed belaying skills.

COMMUNICATION

It's vital that communication be clear between the belayer and the climber. If the wind is blowing, or if the climber is out of earshot, catastrophic errors are possible. If you aren't sure what you've heard, take the more conservative action: Keep the rope on belay, remove any loose slack, and don't ever assume that the climber is no longer in need of the belay. If there is a party of climbers nearby, it's necessary to use first names. We all have seen situations where a climber from one group called "Off Belay" and the belayer from the other party dismantled his own system. Not cool.

Climbers' calls are generally standardized, and all are short and crisp. Don't shout down some long, detailed explanation from 100 feet up. Keep it short and clear. Below are the standard signals. Some apply only to lead climbing.

BELAYER: "On belay. Climb when ready."
The *pledge* has been made.
CLIMBER: "Climbing"
Obvious when on the ground, more critical if there's distance.
CLIMBER: "Up rope"
There's too much slack in the system. Some climbers simply say "Rope." Either way, it means snug it up some. Some say "wake up" if the rope isn't following closely enough.
CLIMBER: "Slack"
The rope is too tight; give me some more. (Can you see now what could happen if the calls weren't precise and the climber said, "There's too much *slack*!"? If all the belayer heard was the last word, there'd be some hard feelings.)
CLIMBER: "Watch me"
I'm in trouble — be alert.
CLIMBER: "Falling!"
No ambiguity here.
CLIMBER: "Tension!"
Usually emphatic. It means take in as

much rope as you can, actually pull and hold me. The beginner says this every few seconds, when "Up rope" would probably be better. The experienced climber just climbs, confident that even if he falls, the belay will hold.
CLIMBER: "Take"
Similar to "Tension!" It means hold me on a tight rope while I rest.
CLIMBER: "*!?*^!?X@!"
You get the picture. Any loud series of nouns and participles generally means that your friend is having a hard time.
BELAYER: "Twenty feet" (or whatever applies)
Not applicable to the top-roper, this one applies to a lead climber who is running short of rope.
CLIMBER: "Off Belay"
He's no longer in need of a belay; you may dismantle your belay if you are *sure* you've heard correctly.
BELAYER: "Again"
Belayer wants to hear it one more time to be absolutely sure.
CLIMBER: "Ready to lower?"
Take in the rope and prepare to hold the weight of the climber.
BELAYER: "Lowering"
You are lowering the climber to the ground. Don't pay out any rope until the climber's weight is on the rope. Otherwise, the climber drops frighteningly before the rope snugs up. Let the rope out slowly and steadily; it helps to judge the speed of your lowering by watching the braid of the rope as it passes through your belay

The good teacher doesn't give move-by-move instruction, but she knows when to offer a timely compelling word of encouragement.

all decorum, challenging the wrath of the deity or even ascribing anatomical functions to inanimate objects. Don't take these rantings literally. Perhaps most satisfying of all is building a partnership so tight that communication is reduced to a few words. With my closest partners, I can function very well with only an "on" or "up" or "OK." With such a partnership, even a gentle tug on the rope sends a clearly understood message. When you begin, however, it's best not to leave such essential communication to chance. Shout it out loud and clear.

device.

BELAYER: "OK" or "Thank You"
I heard and understood your call.

BELAYER: "Off belay"
The rope has been taken out of the belay device and the leader is free to pull up the slack.

At the cliffs or in the gym you might hear a more colorful dialect than the one I have described. Some climbers talk to themselves as a way to keep motivated or calmed. Others, frustrated with failure or nervous about a challenge above, can hold their own with the saltiest sailors. In the heat of the moment, they will lose

LEADING

Leading refers to the method of climbing where both climbers begin at the ground, without the benefit of a top-rope from above. They tie in to opposite ends of the rope, and the leader heads upward, belayed by his partner below. Until the lead climber sets some kind of anchor into the rock, he's unprotected by the rope. The anchors that the leader places and clips into along the way are collectively referred to as *protection*, and the spacing of the anchor points depends on the difficulty of the route, the availability of protection, and the leader's discretion. If he slips, the belayer holds the rope by locking off his belay device, and the leader falls twice the distance between him and his highest protection (plus some extra for slack and rope stretch) until his fall is checked. Once the leader reaches a suitable ledge within the length of his rope, he attaches himself securely to a series of anchor points and belays his partner, the second, who removes and collects the pieces of protection as he climbs. The second on the rope is, in effect, top-roping the pitch; the lead acts as his top anchor.

Unlike top-roping, lead climbing exposes the lead climber to substantial falls even if the anchors are good and to dangerous falls if the anchors are poor or widely spaced. The lead

anchors in an endless variety of situations. Practicing in controlled settings is essential before taking on the real thing.

For some, lead climbing has too many risks; they'd rather concentrate on the sheer gymnastics allowed by a top-rope, or perhaps they haven't the time to maintain the proficiency and judgment

Choose for your early leads routes where protection possibilities are ample and secure.

climber also has huge responsibilities, both for himself and his partner. All his skills and wisdom now come into play: acute judgment about gear and route choice, cleverness in arranging protection points, the endurance needed to both climb *and* protect, and the ability to down-climb from a dangerous situation (no sitting back on the rope here!). Added to this is the responsibility of taking care of a second who is depending on your decisions and capacity to belay well from above. If you do take this end of the rope, you'll need to be able to set up absolutely solid belay

required of a leader. But to most climbers, leading is *real* climbing. The uncertainty that accompanies such a climb multiplies the rewards of its completion.

If you are new to the sport, DO NOT make leading a short-term goal. You've got a long apprenticeship ahead of you, and when you do take the big step, you want to be ready. Be patient and wise as you hone your skills on a top-rope and learn from experienced leaders as you follow them on longer climbs. After becoming a proficient top-roper, your next step is to become a competent second. This means that you'll need a good understanding of the process and at least the basic concepts of problem-solving. No leader wants to drag along a totally dependent partner.

We'll begin our discussion by focusing on what it takes to be a reliable partner accompanying a skilled leader on multi-pitch routes. (For the meaning of italicized terms, see the Glossary, page 179.)

BELAYING AND SECONDING A LEAD CLIMB

Your belaying role is more involved now. The forces that build up in a lead fall can be enormous and can hit you from unexpected directions. If the leader slips off a tiny ledge as he begins, you can be violently jerked downward. If he falls higher up, you could be lifted right up off your feet as the rope is caught by protection above. If he slips while traversing, you could be yanked off to the side. And if a piece of protection fails, the upward force becomes a downward force. And no matter how you are being jerked around, you must also retain a good hold on your brake hand. This is *serious* business.

I confess that my own initiation wasn't so deliberate. We were high on my second multi-pitch climb, and my leader had traversed without protection about 20 feet right from the belay ledge. I fed rope out from a *body belay*, a simple wrap around my

waist, a method I'd never even tested. When he pulled the loose handhold from the cliff and teetered out into space, time seemed for a moment to stop: We looked at each other, he with a broken piece of rock uselessly in his hands and I wondering if this was going to be our end. Somehow I held on and checked the fall. Only later did I notice the deep, oozing groove cut by the climbing rope into my unprotected back.

Belaying the Leader

A good second must be able to hold any kind of lead fall he's subjected

DID YOU KNOW

In the early days before good commercial equipment was available, some ingenious "pitons" were put to use, including wooden blocks, driven into cracks, and stove legs, cut off and drilled to be used on the first ascent of El Capitan. (The long crack system a third of the way up still bears the name "stove leg cracks.") In the 1940s, Swiss ex-patriate John Salathe forged good hard pitons from the axle of a Model-A Ford to tackle some of the high faces in Yosemite National Park.

A belaying disaster: The leader is unaware that his partner's brake hand has left the rope to fiddle with the belay device. Do not let this happen.

to. A leader can't function well unless he's fully confident in his second's abilities. As a belayer, you'll need to pay special heed to most of what your leader does: You'll be paying rope out quickly as he reaches upward to clip a high piece, taking it in gently as he moves up toward the gear, and then paying it out again as he moves beyond. Additionally, you'll need to keep him informed of what's going on below without being a distraction. "Flip the rope over that sharp edge," or "You are on a ground fall," meaning that he needs to put in some protection right away. He might, for example, be 30 feet up a climb with his last protection at 15 feet. Or you

Cleaning the Route

Once the lead climber's belay is established and *only when he has heard "On belay" from above*, the second can take apart and collect the anchor chocks, or unclip the bolts, and begin to climb. His main task here is to *clean* the route, *racking* the gear in an organized fashion so that the next lead can begin without the delay of untangling the mess. *Quick-draws* and chocks are racked on the harness's gear loops, while full-length slings are worn

Your carabiner needs will be slightly different as you become a leader. Lighter weight carabiners and quick-clipping bent-gate carabiners (right) will be useful on longer and harder routes.

Quick-draws for sport routes need to be held stiffly in place for easy clipping. Yet such specialized carabiners aren't versatile enough for general climbing needs.

across the shoulder. Keeping the gear from dangling underfoot will make a big difference as you follow the pitch. Carry along a *nut tool* when you second a climb; it's occasionally necessary for poking loose a stuck chock.

Once at the belay, it is *your* task to tie in (preferably with a figure-8 on a bight. See "Knots," page 120). A good leader will tell you where in the anchor you should clip in (after all, he is the one who has constructed it and understands it), and he will keep you on belay until you are securely fixed to the belay anchor.

After these security measures have been attended to, you can begin giving the leader his gear back — one piece at a time — as he racks up for the next lead.

If all goes well, these will have been your sole responsibilities. If, on

SPECIALIZED CARABINERS

As I begin to describe climbing's varied specialty gear, let me admit that I have a bit of an attitude. I like basic, multi-purpose gear, gear that will let me create ingenious ways to get by with less. Having said that, let's look at some innovative carabiners. Though the basic 'biner shape is functional and effective, some manufacturers keep trying to improve it, and as they do, your options multiply.

One option is known as a *bent-gate* carabiner. It allows a leader to clip in the rope more easily, sometimes even making a move safer because a missed clip would be a disaster. Notice, however, that the feature that makes the clip easy makes an accidental "unclip" easier as well. A falling climber's rope could snag on the gate in such a manner that it unclips itself. I've seen it happen. If you are tempted to buy some bent-gates, understand their limitations, and use them only in situations that call for them.

Another style of carabiner is pre-sewn into a small webbing loop called a *quick-draw* (a unit used to clip a rope into a bolt or other protection). Admittedly, when I saw these for the first time,

continued on page 94

I thought, "What a giant step backwards: a carabiner specifically made not to be versatile." Yet plenty of times when I've been in desperate overhanging territory, where a missed clip means a long fall, these quick-draws seem mighty friendly. They stay put and are easy to clip. Modern sport routes, indoors and out, are often protected solely by pre-placed bolts. In such environments where you won't need to make clever carabiner rappels, pulleys, or ascenders, quick-draws will answer most of your needs. In the mountains, however, be ready to get creative, relying on general-use carabiners to do more with less. The best trick of all is opening a beer bottle with a carabiner. Ask a pro for guidance here.

CARABINER WARNINGS:
A carabiner is designed to be pulled from two directions, not three. If properly oriented, a closed-gate carabiner is reliable.

If improperly loaded (with three or more elements as shown below), its strength is greatly diminished.

Of even greater concern is what we call *gate-loading*, an inadvertent orientation that loads the gate of the 'biner. The tiny pins that hold the gate on are not much thicker than the lead in a pencil, and in this orientation, the carabiner would reliably hold little more than your body weight.

A more esoteric concern is known as *gate chatter* or *whiplash*. When photographed at high speeds, a carabiner gate can sometimes be seen vibrating open as it loads or is banged against the rock. A carabiner must be closed to have full strength, and in crucial situations, many climbers use locking carabiners or doubled and opposed carabiners, see page 78. Some carabiners have a wire gate so light that it doesn't have the mass to vibrate when banged around. These are available from Black Diamond, Omega, Kong, and HB.

the other hand, something goes wrong — the leader is injured, the rope is stuck, you need to make an unplanned descent — then you must be ready to respond. chapter 12, "Preparing for Trouble," is a primer on self-rescue, skills that will surely seem confusing to the beginner but that should be in continual development as you move into the sport. Until you can function independently with such problem-solving, you are too dependent on the leader and the luck that all will go according to plan.

It takes time for the new leader to get used to that insecure feeling of being *above* his gear.

LEADING

Many leaders today begin by climbing pre-protected routes — sport routes — well within their ability level. Such routes won't demand much decision-making, but at least the leader will get used to that unnerving feeling of being above the gear. And it's quite a change:

DID YOU KNOW
Climbers near Dresden, Germany, were so advanced that around the turn of the century they were climbing routes later graded 5.10, a level that wouldn't be reached in America until the 1960s. To protect their routes, they jammed knotted slings into cracks, low-tech and low-impact chocks still in use in some areas.

When you're accustomed to feeling the security of a rope from above, it's eerie to see instead that your lifeline is dangling downward from your waist toward a fragile looking carabiner that you'll swear is a mile below.

Getting used to this feeling is a major part of your transition to lead climbing. You must be able to function under a new reality, knowing that you can't simply sit back for a rest or scream for "Tension!" when you get spooked. Only when you are able to face this calmly will you be able to put in gear, assess its

BOLTS

Bolts are metal shafts inserted into drilled holes in the rock and used as anchor points. The rope is attached by means of a *hanger*. Historically, bolts were notoriously weak and fickle. Stories abound of climbers pulling out rusted, quarter-inch bolts with a simple tug from a sling. Many bolts were placed before there was an accepted standard or research into their application as climbing anchors.

Years ago, I called one of the manufacturers of these ¼-inch bolts to get information about their strength. The engineer with whom I spoke was horrified to learn that I was using them for climbing, telling me that such flimsy anchors were barely strong enough

to hang a pizza sign from a shop-front. He couldn't believe that anyone would be so naive as to use them for life-saving purposes.

Climbers have gotten more sensible, and most of the bolts currently in use are at least ⅜-inch in diameter and generally strong enough to do the job. But most still come from the construction industry, where quality control is inconsistent. Manufacturers generally refuse to endorse their use as life-saving anchors, and most of our information is coming only from the experience of climbers who use them. Added to the variability of the bolt itself is the method by which it is placed. It's impossible to tell from visual inspection whether a bolt is safe (other than obvious looseness or rust). The hole might not be the

security, and manage your rope system.

Make your first leads well within your ability. There will be many kinks (both literal and figurative) to work out as you begin. Learning to lead a rock climb is analogous to learning to drive a car. When we begin, we feel as though we are doing pretty well. But years later, as we look back on our first experiences, we acknowledge that we were in much less control than we realized.

Hours of experience, sprinkled with some close calls, made us better and safer drivers. The same holds for climbing.

On Pre-Protected Routes

If you can see that the route is fully protected by bolts, you'll simply have to figure out how many quick-draws you'll need (plus a couple, figuring that you might fumble and drop one). Talk to your belayer and come to a decision about where he should stand

---

right size, or the bolt might have been under- or over-tightened. Manufacturers have strict guidelines for the use of construction anchors, but there is no authority that regulates the way recreational climbers use them.

Clearly, you won't be placing bolts as you enter the sport. Not only would you be subjecting yourself to risk, but you would be endangering countless others who unwittingly use your anchors later. *Beginners must not place bolts.* They just don't have the necessary experience to do so properly.

Never tap on a bolt with a

hammer to test it. This only damages the bolt. Nor should you crank on a fixed bolt with a wrench. If it's obviously loose, simple tightening may help. But avoid over-tightening, especially if you don't have the experience or even the knowledge of what kind of bolt is in there.

If you choose to lead a bolted sport route, you'll have no choice but to use the gear in place. Make sure, however, that as you anchor the rope for belay, you are into at least two bolt anchors. Never belay, lower, or rappel from a single anchor point.

LOWERING FROM FIXED ANCHORS

If the top anchors of a sport route are fixed with closed rings (not carabiners), you must perform a careful sequence to get your rope safely through before being lowered to the ground. 1) Start by clipping in to the rings with a quick-draw while your belayer keeps you attentively on belay. Pass a bight of rope through the rings. 2) Tie a figure-8 onto that bight and 3) clip back into your harness with a locked carabiner. 4) Now untie, thread the rope through the rings and tie in again. Leave the

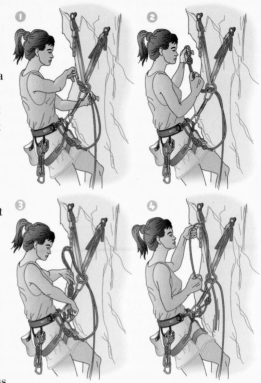

figure-8 clipped to your harness as you lower off; it provides the backup to your new knot.

and anchor, check your harness and tie-in (and those of your belayer). Make sure that your quick-draws are racked where you can reach them, with the lower 'biner gate down and out for easy clipping. If you've already followed or top-roped the pitch, you have a good idea of where you are going to stand to clip into your protection bolts.

Typically (but not always), sport routes are a half rope-length, 80 feet or less to allow for a convenient lowering once the top anchors are clipped. If the route is longer, and your rope is a standard 165 feet, then it won't be possible to lower off with a single rope. It is always essential to have the free end of the rope tied either to a solid anchor or to the belayer's harness so that the unthinkable — losing the end of the rope and dropping the leader — can't happen.

Clipping

Believe it or not, simply clipping your rope into protection carabiners can be frustratingly difficult. When you're scared, every finger feels like a thumb, and the carabiner gate opening seems much narrower than the fat rope you're trying to get in there. The beginner fumbles and fidgets just to get clipped, while a skilled leader can reach down, grab the rope, and drop it cleanly into the 'biner as if there were no gate at all.

The key (I hope you're not tired of hearing this) is practice. Go into

TECHNIQUE TIP

QUICK-CLIPPING TRICKS

There are times when the clip itself can seem the hardest part of the climb; getting the rope finally in place brings on near euphoria. Here are a few tricks of the trade.

Pre-clip a quick-draw onto your rope, with the other 'biner onto your gear loop or even onto your T-shirt. This way, all you have to do is clip the quick-draw to the bolt, without having to clip the rope into the quick-draw in the middle of the move. Use a long and supple quick-draw here in case you inadvertently clip in backwards.

The maneuver described above requires that you pull hard against the rope as you reach the quick-draw higher, which is tough high on a pitch when the rope begins to feel heavy. To eliminate this problem, try rigging a full-length sling (or two) to your rope, with a quick-draw from the top carabiner. You can now safely clip into the bolt, without having to pull against the heavy rope. Once you are in, you are in a more secure position to pull the rope up toward your quick-draw as well.

Sometimes a "cheater stick" is helpful in clipping into the lowest bolt. This allows you to get on the route without the risk of groundfall if that first protection is dangerously high or if the landing is particularly rough. Though there are products on the market for this, you can easily fashion a cheater stick by loosely taping a quick-draw onto a stick with your rope clipped in ahead of time. All you have to do is reach upward with the stick, clip the quick-draw to the bolt, and pull the stick free from the tape. Voila! (Such tactics blend in with top-roping. Be humble later when you boast of your awesome "red-point.")

Perfect clipping technique: middle finger ready to grasp the carabiner while thumb and forefinger snap in the rope. And on overhanging territory like this, you'd better get it right!

approximate the feeling of a real lead, until the clipping becomes habitual. Practice clipping in with your right hand and your left, off to either side, and high above your head. Do it so many times that your fingers develop little brains of their own, and next time you are hanging from a sloping rock edge, your fingers will know what to do.

your basement or garage, or any place where you can hang a quick-draw from a nail or bolt, and do repetitions, with a slightly weighted rope to

There are a few basic clipping methods. The goal of each is to be

Clipping In: Right And Wrong

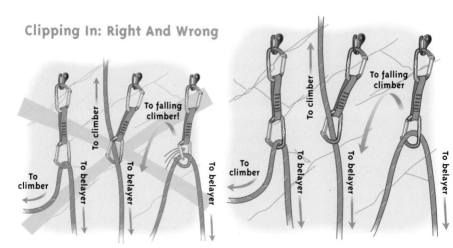

Clip in correctly, leaving the rope exiting from the "top" of the carabiner. Note how the seemingly harmless sequence on the left risks the rope unclipping in a fall.

Right: Wedge-style chocks in a variety of sizes. Note that they are strung with metal wire. **Below:** Black Diamond Hexentrics, the safe, versatile six-sided chocks first developed in the early 1970s by Chouinard Equipment.

efficient and to make sure that the finished clip leaves the rope exiting the 'biner in the right direction. Note that in the illustration (opposite, below) the rope leaves from underneath the carabiner. It looks OK from below, but once you are above, the quick-draw is being twisted, and a fall could drag the rope back across and open the carabiner gate. Longer and more supple quick-draw slings alleviate this problem.

TRADITIONAL LEADING

If you are going to lead traditionally, you'll be out there on natural terrain facing the uncertainty of route-finding and less-than-perfect rock, placing your own protection, setting up your own anchors, and figuring out how you are going to get down. You must be much more conservative under these conditions because you aren't just going bolt-to-bolt but instead could find yourself off-route or way out

?

DID YOU KNOW

The first chocks were actually small stones jammed in cracks and tied off with slings as anchor points. Later, British climbers used six-sided machine nuts looped with cord. The six-sided shape still can be seen in the Hexentric chocks found on many climbers' racks.

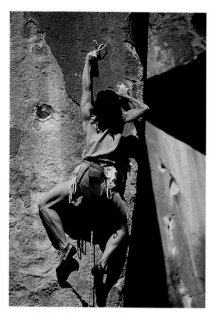

A stiff quick-draw gives you a few precious inches of reach.

routes with ample protection possibilities, preferably routes you've already climbed on a top-rope. Give yourself the opportunity to work on the mechanical side of the process without having to worry about the climbing moves themselves.

Protection

If the route isn't fixed with protection gear, you'll be placing your own — one of the most satisfying elements of traditional climbing. Your rack will depend quite a bit on the kind of rock and the particular demands of the route. It doesn't make much sense, for example, to carry large pieces of gear when the pitch is a thin crack leading to a tree-covered ledge. When the territory is unknown, however, you must carry a wide variety of protection. An overview of the most widely used protection devices follows:

PASSIVE WEDGES OR CHOCKS The simplest of all protection, and in

from your last good piece of protection. Such traditional leading certainly presents more hazardous variables, but at the same time, it offers remarkably gratifying rewards.

Choose your early leads on easy

TECHNIQUE TIP

TRAINING WHEELS FOR NOVICE LEADERS

There are a few ways you can cover yourself as you gain proficiency as a leader. Most obvious is simply to "pretend" you are leading, trailing a rope and setting protection as you climb. All the while, however, you'll remain on another top-rope from above.

A slightly less secure method is to either pre-set some or all of the protection, or instead, to hang a separate rope with tied loops every five or ten feet so that you can clip these as well as your own protection, just in case your placements aren't secure.

many ways the best, are passive wedges. Since their use is so obvious and they are so easy to inspect, these will be fundamental to your protection system. When pitons went out of general use in the 1970s, the first artificial chocks were simple wedge-shaped blocks of aluminum slung with either stout cord or wire cable. The idea was simple: The block wedged into a constriction in a crack, making an anchor point as strong as the cord or wire itself.

Such wedges took on two generic names at first. Artificial *chock stones*, or *chocks*, refers to their similarity to the keystone in masonry, such as the

A well-placed wired chock. Note, however, that it is directional; it only holds when the direction of force is from below.

center block in your own arching fireplace mantel. In fact, climbers

TECHINQUE TIP

HINTS FOR PLACING CHOCKS

● Set up your rack (see page 104) for easy access. Know where everything is and how to get it off your rack fast without dropping anything. Color-coding helps here.

● Pick the size smaller than the one you initially guessed; beginners have a tendency to choose a size too large when they are learning the craft.

● Vibrate the chock gently as you let it "find" its best placement. Don't just set it in and jerk it tight. Instead, the slight shaking helps it "drive" around in the subtle irregularities of the crack to find its most secure spot. I joke that I place better gear after I've had a couple of cups of strong coffee.

● Pull the sling downward and outward a bit to test how it is going to react to such forces. The downward force is obvious — don't neglect positioning the piece so as to resist outward force as well.

● Place larger pieces — Hexes, for example — with your fingers right on the nut. Smaller, wired nuts can be inserted by holding the wire alone.

had long used natural chock stones, rocks wedged into cracks which could be slung with cord to create an anchor point. Large and solidly wedged blocks can be quite safe. Climbers also experimented with carrying some smaller rocks in their pockets to wedge along the way. A few climbers fell on such contrived protection, but they added at least some degree of security for the early climbers.

In Britain, the story goes, clever climbers would find machine nuts strewn along the railroad tracks that led near their climbs. By stringing a cord through the center hole, they were able to create strong metal chock stones to be used as removable wedges. Thus, the chocks took on the name *nuts*. In 1971, Chouinard Equipment introduced the Hexentric, a six-sided chock based somewhat on the original machine-nut shape, to complement the "Stopper," its own version of the wedge-shaped chock.

Climbers will refer to all such

RACKING GEAR FOR THE LEAD

There are two basic modes of racking gear: on a sling draped over your shoulder and across your chest, or from gear loops on the waist belt of your harness. The shoulder rack has the advantage of being easily transferable as two climbers switch leads. The waist-rack feels more stable, lacking the swinging weight of the over-shoulder gear. In fact, most climbers use a combination of the two, a method that evolves for each climber, and one that allows ease of locating and removing individual pieces.

Slings, or "runners," are best slung over your shoulder and across your chest, but don't

"bury" them by placing your gear sling on top of them and in the other direction or by putting on your backpack over them. Quick-draws and free carabiners

anchors as either chocks or nuts; they'll loosely assign the term *stopper* to any wedge-shaped chock, adopting Chouinard's (now Black Diamond's) brand name, or *Hex* to refer specifically to Black Diamond's excellent six-sided chock.

The use of the wedged-shape chock is quite clear: Place it into a narrowing crack and make sure that it has good surface contact and can resist the direction of impact you anticipate. If the rock is sound and the placement secure, then the

Take full advantage of the Hex's ability to cam by placing it wide-side-up in any horizontal or diagonal crack. Otherwise, the versatile chock becomes just a simple space-filler.

are best racked on the waist.

Although it's possible, and sometimes preferable, to rack just one chock per carabiner, larger racks make this impractical. Use this method only if you can see that the pitch requires some fast placements and clipping. Otherwise, it's best to rack according to size: Each carabiner holds three or four corded chocks of the same general size, with wire chocks as many as eight to the carabiner.

Unless you're really confident about choosing the right size first try, you'll be better off taking the entire carabiner off, then experimenting for the right chock before even taking it from the carabiner. Once the chock is successfully in place, you can remove the whole 'biner (and other chocks) before

adding the quick-draw or runner. This is especially useful with the wired chocks. When you are in a tight place, you'll discover that your teeth are another set of fingers as you pick out the chocks without letting go of your hold on the wall.

Spring-loaded camming devices are cumbersome enough to warrant one-piece-per-carabiner racking.

Whatever your method, let it be one that works for you and that is easily transferable to your partner if you are to alternate leads. Some compromise might be necessary here as you develop partnerships. Color-coding helps as you buy cordage for your chocks. Continually refine your racking system until it is as clean and useful as you can make it.

STRINGING CHOCKS

In the past, the rule was to string your chocks with the strongest (read thickest) cord you could fit. The big chocks could carry a hefty 8- or 9-mm cord, while the medium ones got 7-mm. Smaller than that wasn't safe, so these chocks were rigged with steel cable.

With the advent of the super-strong thin cords like Kevlar, Spectra, and Gemini, all but the smallest nuts can get a full-strength cord. In fact, newer chocks are drilled small to accept these super-cords.

A chock will need 3 to 3½ feet of 5.5-mm Spectra or its equivalent tied with a triple fisherman's knot. Remember, 5.5 nylon or Perlon wouldn't be strong enough. The triple fisherman's knot instead of the traditional double fisherman's is required to hold the especially slippery Spectra fibers. The finished product will be a loop about 10 to 12 inches long. Longer is cumbersome to rack; shorter inhibits usefulness and requires more runners and quick-draws.

weakest link will be the cord or cable.

The Hexentric is a good and simple chock design. Not only does it wedge into a constriction like any chock, but it cams, or rotates as it is loaded. This camming allows the Hex to make the most of whatever constriction the crack offers, working even in a crack whose sides are nearly parallel. It takes experience to fully appreciate the options offered by the Hex; experimentation is necessary here. Keep a few things in mind though: Take full advantage of the camming action by placing the largest surface upward whenever possible. In a diagonal or horizontal crack, the direction the cord pulls will rotate the nut and augment the security of the placement. Placed large-side-down in the same crack, the Hex will be more like a simple chock.

Notice also that each Hex has a larger size option if you simply rotate it to its wider configuration. This does, however, offer less surface area in contact with the rock and thus less security. Finally, as with stopper-type chocks, an end-to-end placement creates another option, though again with much less surface area.

The narrower the crack or the more obvious the constriction, the more likely it is you will use a wedge-shaped chock. Larger cracks, or cracks with more nearly parallel sides, are the territory of the Hex. In general, the larger the nut, the more

NON-DIRECTIONAL PROTECTION

Anchors are considered either "directional" or "non directional," depending on whether they can withstand pulls from a variety of directions. This distinction is important as you plan your rope line and anticipate the forces that might be generated on lower pieces if you fall high above. Chocks are typically directional. A chock that can hold a moose might be lifted from its placement by a gentle tug from above. (I even saw one blown from its crack by wind!)

Directional chocks can be combined to create non-directional anchors. Chocks used together in "opposition" become a single non-directional anchor. Beware, however, that in many opposition configurations, failure of either chock means failure of the combination. In other words, the two chocks aren't twice as secure, they're twice as likely to fail. It's best to have such chock opposition set so that the opposition piece is used to assist another piece, but so that the main chock isn't fully dependent on the directional piece below it. The clove-hitched sling (bottom) does this, making the pair much more secure than in the top set up.

Bolts and most pitons, as well as slings girth-hitched on trees or natural chock stones, can be considered non-directional.

The two "directional" chocks work together to form a single anchor. The bottom config-uration is better than the one above, because the two chocks are held in place with a clove-hitch, keeping some tension between the chocks and making both some-what independent anchors.

Left: Don't let the camming unit "umbrella" in a crack that's too wide; it has no holding power.
Right: If you must use a rigid-stemmed Friend in a horizontal crack, it helps to cord it off short with Spectra to reduce leverage and protect the stem from breaking or bending under load.

realistic it is to rely on its end-to-end placement. Larger chocks simply have more surface area and holding power.

Wedge-shaped chocks are most often slung with wire cable, though it is possible to buy unwired chocks in the larger sizes to sling yourself with cord. Hexes need the

Spring-loaded camming devices come with three or four cams, manipulated by a trigger mechanism.

flexibility of cord to take full advantage of their camming power: That's why the smallest Hexes, those on wire cable, are less popular than the larger ones.

ACTIVE CAMMING UNITS In the late 1970s a strange and futuristic device appeared and changed the climbing world forever. Unlike the clean lines and obvious function of the chock, the active camming unit (or spring-loaded camming device) looked all springs and wheels. Traditionalists were aghast, vowing never to be wooed by such technology.

Innovators knew a good thing when they saw it and quickly added it to their rack.

The Friend, created by Ray Jardine and produced and marketed by Wild Country, is based on earlier camming experiments, but is the first to gain wide use. It works by taking

ROCK CLIMBING

advantage of the principles of camming. Four independent cams on a single axle work together to anchor in a crack. The harder you pull, the more the cams are forced outward and the tighter they hold. Finally, a piece of gear that doesn't even require a bottleneck constriction to hold. A parallel-sided

When a chock gets stuck in a crack, you'll be glad you thought to bring along a nut tool.

crack is no problem. These devices even work in slightly flaring cracks.

Over the years, climbers have

FIXED GEAR

Climbers refer to any protection or anchors left in place as fixed. This isn't to imply that the gear is reliable; it only means that it's been left by earlier climbers who either deemed it helpful to the route or simply couldn't remove it after using it. In addition to the bolts discussed above, you'll come across fixed pitons (a.k.a. "pegs" or "pins"). Often these are placed in cracks too thin for chocks and left in place by design. Sometimes they are remnants from an earlier age before chocks were used.

Even though pitons can be solid, you should treat them with suspicion. Pitons will loosen up with age, either because the crack has widened owing to erosion or to the piton's rusting deep within the crack. Even the best-looking pitons can be disintegrated. In wet areas like the Northeast, the

pitons may be continuously wet as they stick into the moist dirt deep in the crack. I have a collection of over 50 pitons that I have removed by hand; some just wiggled out easily, others that seemed solid on the outside were almost fully rusted away inside. As a leader, you'll be happy to clip a fixed piton (it's better than nothing), but whenever possible, back it up with your own gear.

Fixed chocks are also common, though seldom installed deliberately. Most likely, they were stuck or overlooked by an earlier party, and you are free to remove them as you go. Wire cables on fixed chocks rust and weaken, especially inside the chock where the moisture remains and where it's difficult to inspect. Cords in chocks quickly break down from exposure to sunlight. Don't expect such cables or cords to be safe.

The leader has used longer slings under the overhang to reduce rope drag. Can you picture the resistance he would face if he had clipped in short?

for shallower and narrower placements and have also become a standard. While the typical rack of the 1970s might have contained corded wedges and Hexes, today's rack consists most commonly of wired wedges and spring-loaded camming devices.

Active-Camming Primer

The active-camming unit is remarkable, but, as with all gear, its reliability depends on how it is used. It pays to work hard to understand its uses and limitations. Some things to remember are:

① Solid stems may bend or break in horizontal placements; thread a cord to reduce leverage on a Friend stem.
② Make sure the crack is clean and crystal-free. This is especially important when placing smaller units, where any dirt or breakage of crystals in the crack could allow the cams to open too wide.

grown increasingly reliant on such spring-loaded camming devices (SLCDs), though a few changes have been introduced since the original Friend. The first units were built on a solid aluminum stem, good for directing the load to the cams, but limited in horizontal cracks where the stem could be bent or broken in a hard fall. Flexible units became the answer for this. Even in a horizontal placement, the wire cables bend with the force and remain intact.

Three-cam units (TCUs) are used

❸ Align the unit in the direction of anticipated load. Too many climbers stick the device straight into a vertical crack when, in fact, the load from a fall would be downward.

❹ Don't allow the cams to fully open, or "umbrella." Most units have virtually no holding power in this position. Only Black Diamond's Camalot, due to its unique dual-axle design, is designed to hold in such a fully-opened position.

❺ If a cam is fully closed when it's inserted into the crack, it will be nearly impossible to remove.

❻ Watch for "walking." If a four-cam

The leader's arrangement of protection becomes vital for the second only on traverses. If the second falls after having unclipped the high piece, he'll wind up dangling in space, unable to get back on the rock (see "Climbing the Rope," page 154 for the solution to this problem).

unit stem or wire is wiggled back and forth, the whole unit will gradually creep into the crack as first one set of cams, and then the other, grabs. Use long slings as flexible extensions to counter this wiggle tendancy, or if possible, place the camming device hard against the back of the crack to hold it in place. At best, the walking will cost you the piece. At the worst, the device will walk into an opening inside the crack and umbrella, rendering it useless. Such a clearly constricting crack might be better suited to a passive piece like a Hex or wedge.

ON THE PITCH

Leading is a thinking person's game: Where does the route go? What's my next protection going to be? Is my rope running straight and free of sharp edges and loose rock? Where's the next belay? Am I considering my second as I set up my protection on traverses? In other words, the leading game is multifaceted and all-absorbing, and you'll have to stay especially alert.

Using Slings (or Runners)

As you set and arrange your protection, you'll have to decide whether you are going to "clip short" with a carabiner or a quick-draw, or "clip long" with a full-length sling (or more). Your initial temptation will be to clip short so that your fall length is minimized. Single carabiner clips are acceptable ONLY if you are sure that they won't run the risk of coming unclipped as the rope runs back over the carabiner gate in a fall or traverse. It's much more likely that you will choose to use a quick-draw, a short sling joining two carabiners. Such a unit provides a flexible extension and greatly reduces the chance of the carabiner inadvertently opening during the lead. Most sport routes are climbed using quick-draws at each bolt. (Don't steal the draws if you come upon a route that is pre-equipped when you arrive.)

If your route is going to wander, or if you suspect that gear might be pulled out by the rope, then you must

GEAR TALK

DID YOU SAY KILONEWTONS?

The impacts and strengths you'll encounter in the climbing world are metric. A kilogram is equal to approximately 2.2 pounds. A newton is the unit of force required to move a mass of one kilogram one meter per second per second. Climbing gear is generally rated in kiloNewtons (kN) since it doesn't really hold a static weight, but instead changes the inertia of a mass. One kiloNewton, then, is a force of approximately 220 pounds. A carabiner rated to, say, 24 kN will resist a force of over 5,000 pounds.

use full-length or longer runners. A wandering rope line will pull on protection gear from unanticipated directions. Sometimes chocks can lift out from rope-drag alone. And more serious, if you fall, the outward pull

Clever equalization and opposition of chocks can create strong, multi-directional anchors.

will be even harder and could rip out every chock except your highest. If it were to fail, you'd be history.

ROPE DRAG Rope drag is another consequence of clipping too short or arranging a rope line that wanders. If you aren't careful early on with your use of runners, then high on the pitch the drag of the rope will feel as if your partner were hanging from it. (It's like climbing a hard, unprotected face dragging a 50-pound bag of potatoes.) Rope drag can become a real nightmare. And despite my warnings, you'll probably create such a situation as you learn to lead. That experience will be your best teacher of all.

When in doubt, err on the side of longer runners. Almost all wire-cabled chocks (they're really stiff) need at least a quick-draw as a flex-ible extension. Most corded chocks and spring-loaded camming devices also need at least a quick-draw unless the line of the climb is unusu-ally straight. The added length of the fall you'd face by adding quick-draws or runners is usually less serious than the consequences of the gear pulling out from having been clipped too short.

Consider Your Second

If the line is straight, your second won't care about how you protect the pitch beyond the obvious pieces early on to protect the belay. If, however, the line traverses, the second could be placed in a perilous position by the careless leader. Consider this scenario: You face a hard move fol-lowed by a long, easy, traverse ledge. You put in solid gear, make the move,

Here the exposed second will face only a dunking if he slips. But the leader must always consider the risks of the second as he places protection on a traverse.

and then hike across, knowing that you really don't need protection for this horizontal cruise. Your second comes up, has to remove the gear and *then* make the hard move, looking at a horrendous fall if he slips.

The leader must always consider what the situation for the second will be, and as a rule, there must be good protection *after* every hard move on a traverse. As a leader, you must not expose your second to a dangerous fall.

Clever use of double ropes can help in such situations, but realistically, few teams employ double ropes and so face such situations with one rope alone. If, after all options are explored, it's clear that the second (or weaker) climber must be exposed

to a long fall, there remain some useful (albeit imperfect) options.

❶ The second can leave the gear in place, extend the runner, make the hard move to safety, and then reach back across to clean the gear.

❷ The second can stay clipped in, ask for some slack, and practice the move a few times until he's sure he's got it. Then he can clean the protection and go for it.

❸ The team can agree to sacrifice the gear. The second stays clipped in, asks for slack, and makes the move to security. He then grabs the rope leading to the leader, ties a figure-8 on a bight, and clips it to his harness (two opposed locking 'biners). He can then untie his own knot and pull the rope through, leaving the gear behind.

Although such options are available, it's better not to put yourself into such a jam in the first place. It's the leader's job not to jeopardize his second.

Anchoring at the Belay

When the leader has reached a suitable belay — ideally, a good, flat stance with ample anchor potential — he must construct an anchor that is redundant and allows for no extensions should any single piece fail (see page 73 for R.E.N.E.). Beginners somehow manage to construct the most complex anchors imaginable, with slings going off in every conceivable direction. Better to keep it simple, and no method beats the *cordalette* for this.

A cordalette is a long loop of strong cordage (7-mm Perlon or 5.5 Spectra, Gemini, or other super-

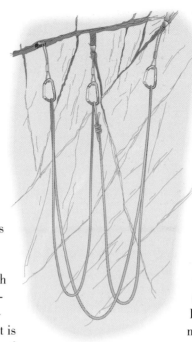

A cordalette is the quickest and simplest tool for creating a "hard point" for anchoring at the belay. Clip each piece of the anchor, bring the loops down in the anticipated direction of load, and tie them off using a figure-8 or overhand on a bight. The resulting loop is redundant, and the loads are relatively equal on each of the anchor points.

cord) tied into a loop with a double-fisherman's knot (or triple for Spectra and other slippery fibers). Eighteen to 20 feet is most useful, making a loop that if quadrupled is the same length as your other runners and can be carried over your shoulder, kept even by a carabiner.

Although the cordalette has numerous uses, its best one is bringing several anchor points together to form a single "hard point," a double or triple loop that links and virtually equalizes the anchor points.

Equalized Sling: Correct, the sliding X. Incorrect, disaster. The loads are equalized, but failure on either side means failure of both.

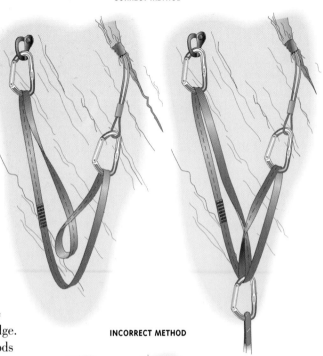

CORRECT METHOD

INCORRECT METHOD

If the leader can create a sensible, single hard-point anchor, then it's much easier to belay safely, and the second will have no trouble tying in when he arrives at the ledge.

Other methods work as well, but without the tidiness of the cordalette. Slings can be folded and knotted to adjust them into relative equalization. The "sliding X" can be used as part of the anchor, though remember that if one piece fails, the system is shock-loaded, and that a single X'ed sling isn't redundant; it needs another sling in like fashion.

If there's a strong tree at the belay, then the simplest method of all is for the leader to walk around the tree and tie a figure-8 on a bight clipped back to his harness. It's secure, simple, and gear free.

BELAYING THE SECOND

Your task now is to belay your second as he cleans the pitch. Yet the job is a tougher one than presented in the slingshot belay you learned as a top-roper. A second falling on a top belay can create surprising forces, and you've got to be ready. Most important is that you find a solid position: Sitting is ususally best, but with proper positioning, a standing belay can be effective.

Be ready to transfer the load right to your solid belay anchors. That is best accomplished by belaying both through the belay loop of your harness *and* the the tie-in loop of your rope. Make sure the length of your tie-in is exact so that you won't be pulled off balance as you absorb the impact of the fall. The clove hitch's adjustability makes this a popular

Belaying a second straight down from the belay. A second falling on this spectacular Devil's Tower climb will load the belayer and the anchors directly. This method requires exact positioning of the belay to withstand such direct loading. Compare with the photograph on page 118.

knot at the belay (see "Knots," page 122).

Not only must you be ready to

catch a fall, but you must be in a position to hold a dangling climber for as long as it takes for him to get ready for another try or even prusik up the rope if need be. Plan for such a load by standing or sitting solidly in the direction of anticipated loading, and make sure your tie-in length is exact.

If guide Dennis Goode falls here on New Hampshire's difficult *Camber* (5.11), his belayer gets pulled UP to security because he has redirected the belay load back up through the anchor.

E S S E N T I A L
K N O T S

In this chapter I've included most of the knots climbers use. In the beginning, you'll want to know just a few knots and know them well. This is far better than trying to remember a dozen but never being quite sure of any of them.

Knots are evaluated according to four criteria:

SECURITY Does the knot stay tied reliably?

STRENGTH Every time you bend a rope under stress, you've slightly weakened the rope. All knots bend the rope, and so all knots reduce to a degree the strength of the rope in which they are tied. In the days of

natural-fiber ropes, this was an important consideration. With the advent of nylon and the newer materials like Kevlar and Spectra, the "strength" of a knot is seldom questionable.

SYMMETRY Is the knot so visibly clean and obvious that there's no mistaking it? Some knots are harder to "see" than others, and in the beginning at least, you ought to stick with the symmetrical ones.

TIGHTENING UNDER LOAD How easy will it be to untie the knot after it's been heavily loaded?

Knots are of a few general categories. You'll see *retraced* knots.

These begin with a knot put into a single strand to be followed — retraced — by the second strand as the knot is completed. Also, you will get to know knots tied *on a bight* (doubled loop of rope); such knots create good quick links for clipping into anchors.

Purists distinguish between *bends* (what the rest of us would call knots) and *hitches* (loops involving single strands of rope wrapped around something). We can put this distinction aside and call the whole bunch knots — with apologies to the sailors.

OVERHAND ON A BIGHT This one is easy to tie and inspect; its only down side is that it's hard to untie after it has been loaded. For this reason, climbers use a figure-8 in most cases where an overhand would work.

FIGURE-8 ON A BIGHT Secure, strong, symmetrical. It's easy to tie, and it won't freeze up if it's loaded heavily. This knot is one of the essentials of rock-climbing.

RETRACED FIGURE-8 This allows you to connect the figure-8 on a bight directly to an object, like a tree, and it is the best knot for attaching a rope to your harness. In essence, you're tying one half of the knot, running your rope around the object, and then retracing to complete it.

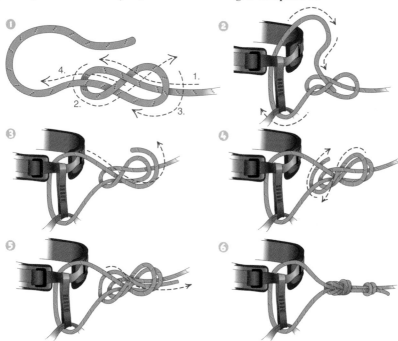

WATER KNOT Also known as a Ring Bend or a Retraced Overhand. This is the preferred knot for webbing. It allows the flat material to lie without folding. It's symmetrical and strong, yet not very secure unless tightened carefully. *Check water knots in webbing frequently and be sure to leave at least an inch of "tail" after tightening.* Such a knot works in rope as well, but it isn't as secure as the double-fisherman's (see page 122).

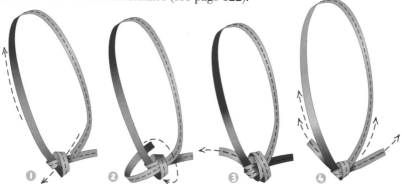

DOUBLE FISHERMAN'S Also known as a "grapevine" knot, this works graphically by having two knots block on each other. The result is a symmetrical double-X design, easy to inspect. It is the most secure way you can join two ropes or ends of cords for slings. But once loaded, it's hard to untie. Prusik cords tied with a double fisherman's will be more or less "welded" in place after a few uses. Rappel lines tied with this knot can be worked loose with a little effort once you're safely on the ground. Keep the X's lined up for symmetry. One half of the double-fisherman's makes the best back-up knot to be used in conjunction with other climbing knots.

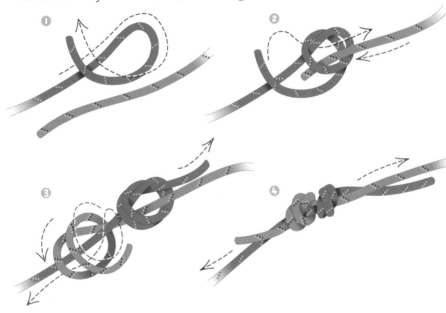

CLOVE HITCH The beauty of this one is that it allows easy adjustment without your having to dismantle the knot. When at a belay, for example, the leader who uses a clove hitch to fix his rope to the anchor carabiners can readily adjust his positioning so that he can belay most effectively. If he had tied a figure-8 on a bight, he would have a harder time adjusting and might be tempted to belay without the exact anchor length needed to do the best job.

The clove hitch is, however, very fickle. If it isn't cinched down tight, it can ride up the carabiner gate and open the 'biner. Not good. Note also how it loads the carabiner (shown in Figure 3). If it is backwards, the strength of the carabiner will be compromised because it is being loaded out away from the "elbow" of the 'biner. Use doubled, opposed carabiners to eliminate this danger. The clove hitch works well to link several anchor points, but you'd still be wise to include a "hard knot" like a figure-8 or overhand as part of any anchor system using clove hitches.

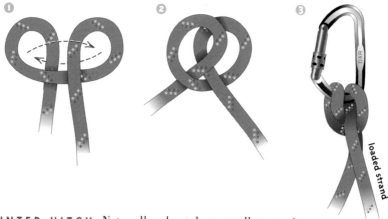

MUNTER HITCH Not really a knot, but actually a moving belay hitch, essential if you drop your belay device. I include it here because of its close relationship to the clove hitch.

PRUSIK This and the following *friction knot* are made from a thinner cord or sling wrapped around a thicker rope. When tensioned, they grab onto the line and are useful in a variety of situations. They are, however, fairly fickle: The knots could slip if you don't put on enough wraps, and any slippage could result in heat, melting the thin cord. In general, knots like the prusik hold better when the cord is thinner and more supple and when the rope is thicker, softer, and fuzzier.

The knot doesn't work well with webbing. It needs 6-mm or 7-mm cord to hold well on a 10-mm to 11-mm rope.

The prusik needs three wraps on a single rope and two wraps on a doubled rope (as in a rappel). Make sure that the knot is cleanly tied; any mess here will greatly reduce its holding power.

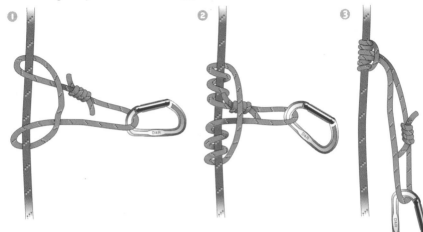

KLEIMHEIST This is the preferred knot when your only material is flat webbing. Tied with $^{11}/_{16}$-inch nylon webbing, the knots hold pretty well. With Spectra slings, the slipperiest of all, the knot needs at least five full wraps to be sure. The knot is hard to loosen after loading, and when it starts to grab, it binds up quite a bit — an irritation but not a danger to the rappeller who is using it as a backup.

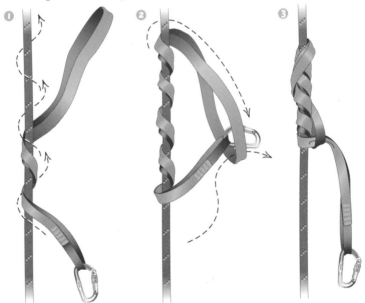

MOVING
FROM GYM
TO REAL ROCK

I knew the future had arrived when, clicking through the TV channels, I recognized the skyline of my hometown, Providence, Rhode Island, as a backdrop to a towering climbing wall. ESPN was staging the Extreme Games, and there in the Eastern flatlands were the world's top sport climbers surrounded by a phalanx of reporters and baggy-pantsed groupies oohing and ahhing over stars like Hans Florine and Katie Brown as they climbed their way to thrilling victories and etched into America's consciousness like never before the sport of climbing. Not quite the scene I remember reading about during my own early days as a climber.

Twenty-five years ago, we heard weird stories coming out of what was then the USSR and Eastern Europe about rock-climbing races. Absurd! Climbing was an experience, not a competition. Surely such events would never happen over here! And then came the artificial climbing wall, in its first incarnation, a series of simple wooden handholds bolted onto garage walls for fun and training in the off-season. As the number of indoor walls grew, so did the number of climbers who favored them. In time, the fabricated climbing wall would no longer be seen as a substitute for real climbing, but as a genuine sport of its own.

While not a climbing wall, a fingerboard is easily installed above a doorway and provides excellent training while off the rock.

Today, there are climbing gyms in most major American cities, and although their concentration is still greatest near the established rock-climbing centers, climbing is becoming available even to a population who has never been to the hills. For kids, youth climbing programs can rival Little League, and a wall workout is fast replacing lunch-hour handball for a growing number of urban professionals. Parents are even hosting birthday parties for neighborhood kids at the local gym. Sure beats hiring a clown.

You don't have to have any experience or equipment to get a taste of climbing at today's indoor climbing centers. Most gyms have gear available and offer clinics or private instruction to introduce you to the

BUILD YOUR OWN WALL

Maybe there's no nearby climbing wall, or perhaps you just want a hard workout right in your own home. Indoor wall construction is easy. You need a space, a few sheets of plywood, a smattering of holds, and basic carpentry skills.

The construction is fairly simple. Bolt some holds onto a sheet of ¾-inch plywood, and you have a climbing wall. Maybe it won't be as impressive as the one on the Snowbird Lodge or as exotic as the one in New York's Reebok gym with its two genuine palm trees. But, hey, you're just looking for a workout and some fun.

The simplest surfaces are the vertical ones like your basement or garage wall. The stud framing is already in place, and all you have to do is install the plywood. But simple vertical surfaces soon loose their appeal as the wall begins to feel too easy.

Your attic might be a better bet. Here, the roof naturally overhangs and often has interesting angles created by dormers and other features. The more variety you can build into the wall the better. If you have no such surfaces at your disposal, you can still frame in a climbing wall. Just make sure that it is strong, with 2 by 6s spaced 16 inches on center for stiffness. And resist using thinner than ¾-inch plywood.

Any space can be converted into a good training ground. Here plywood sheets dotted with artificial holds turn an attic into a playground of angles and overhangs.

basics of harnesses, knots, and belay methods. Most facilities will also work you toward some level of tested proficiency before letting you climb and belay on your own. Expect each gym to have firm policies about technique: They'll mandate a particular belay method, and even if it's slightly different from techniques you've learned in this book or gleaned from experienced climbers, the gym staff will want you to follow their rules to the letter.

Although crude wooden hand- and footholds provide good exercise, store-bought holds, with their endless shapes and easy installation, are much better. Manufactured holds are attached to the wall by bolts that screw into threaded inserts called T-nuts, available with the purchase of holds and also from most construc-

tion supply houses. Install the T-nut inserts at about a one-foot grid before you put up the plywood; it's better to have too many than too few because, once the wall is built, you can't add more unless you leave access to the back of the wall.

Most climbing stores sell holds in packs of five or ten, but you'll probably get a better deal by shopping in the climbing magazines and ordering by mail. You'll want variety: small ones low on the wall to develop foot-work, medium-size holds for hard finger work, and big guys for developing arm, shoulder, and back muscles and for the plain fun of swinging like a monkey high on the wall. The modular nature of the holds allows you to turn them at a variety of angles or swap them around as you continually change your surface. And don't

Gym climbing can get serious. The competition circuit is growing as climbers vie for high rankings and sponsorships.

ings and sponsorship on the line. Currently, there is a World Cup Tour, and it looks as though the sport will be in the Olympics before long. But don't be deterred by the hype and glitz of the big time. Find out about a local event that is geared to your level and have fun.

forget safety. Some old mattresses scattered on the floor make for a much softer landing. Even a short fall can do real damage when you are out of position and off balance.

Competitions

Try a competition at your local wall. You'll be surprised to see that egos are manageable and that you aren't the only neophyte willing to give it a shot. Competitions for newcomers are top-roped on courses set according to various levels of difficulty and designated by colored tapes at the holds. Between rounds, you'll have to wait out of sight of the wall; no competitor should have the advantage of previewing or watching another climber's sequences. Judging is fairly easy: Whoever gets highest wins.

The pro circuit is another matter. Here, the stakes are high, with rank-

Other Games to Play

You can have friendly competitions even at your own tiny homemade wall. There's Vertical Tennis, where one person "serves" by pointing out a sequence of handholds from the ground and then jumps on, hoping to make good. If he gets it and the others don't, score one point. If he blows it, he loses his serve. The strategy becomes cutthroat as each server tries to exploit the weaknesses of the other. Reach moves become the sequence design of the taller climber. Low, squatty traverses are the ace card of the short and agile. Bet a six-pack on it (domestic for regular season, imported for the playoffs), and you'll all be that much more inspired.

Then there is the Add-On game, where one climber does a short sequence and the other climber repeats the sequence and adds a move. As the move sequences grow longer, endurance and "muscle memory" improve, keys to success on hard routes. There is no doubt that as you milk your own wall for all it can offer, you will discover good games of your own to keep the experience fresh and your skills building.

Competition climbing is done either on a top-rope (as shown) or on the lead with preplaced protection bolts and quick draws. While the sight of a falling leader may excite a crowd, most beginner and novice events are wisely held with the security of the top-rope.

Moving to Real Rock

If you begin your climbing experience in the gym and wish to try it on real stone, get ready for some initial frustrations. Climbing walls are built for just that, and the spacing and position of handholds and footholds are established with climbers in mind. Not so with real rock, where the cliff is just a cliff and it is up to the climber to figure out how (or if) it's possible to climb. While the indoor wall is a creation adjusted to our wishes, rock requires that we do the adjusting.

You'll find the footwork on actual rock to be your biggest challenge. The artificial surface is dotted with bolt-on holds, and it's pretty obvious what your options are. Look at actual rock as one big foothold; that is, don't limit your footwork to specific and obvious holds. Instead, consider the whole surface and ways you can smear and friction a foot where the surface is not quite a hold but little more than a rough spot. Accordingly, you'll be well-served if you take smaller steps between holds rather than try to make the awkward and unproductive high step to the good ledge.

Accustomed to the vertical and overhanging routes on plastic, you may be thrown off by equally difficult but much lower-angled rock. Indoors, your eyes scanned upwards for handholds, and your body position was generally geared toward resting on straight arms while you transferred the weight to your feet. With the rock less than vertical and the handholds less accommodating, you'll need to bend forward more at the waist, lower your hands, and stare more intently at your feet for progress. Some rock climbs are indeed overhanging, and here your gym background will serve you well. But when the rock is less steep, the subtleties of footwork and balance take on greater importance than arm power and endurance.

As you've heard before, don't get hung up in grades and numbers. You may be able to power off a 5.10 on plastic but find that a natural 5.7 face climb looks like an inclined mirror. Don't be discouraged. It's a different world, and the number comparisons just don't do it justice.

Leading: Indoors and Out

Gym owners want you to have fun, but they don't want to hear from your lawyer. And so they space their protection bolts conservatively, often less than five feet apart. In many ways, leading on plastic is little more than moving your top-rope higher and higher as you go. It's still harder than top-roping, but it can lull you into thinking that leading is no big deal.

SPORT ROUTES

On an outdoor sport route, the bolts may be close together at logical rests that allow safe and easy clipping. Or they may be frighteningly distant from each other and at inconvenient locations. If the route is installed on rappel and if the bolter has practiced the route and thought hard about just where the bolts need to go, then the experience might be more like the gym. If, however, the route was done traditionally from the ground up, the bolts will likely be less predictable and convenient. Make your judgments carefully before heading up into such unknown terrain, and learn some of the clever panic-clipping methods discussed on page 99.

With a good belay, an indoor fall should be perfectly safe. The rope won't be running over sharp rock edges, and you won't be smashing into a ledge on your way down. Outdoors, you'll find a host of new variables to turn what could have been a soft catch into a painful and dangerous crash.

TRADITIONAL ROUTES

So far, we've compared the gym only to the pre-protected sport routes outdoors. Traditional leading is much more serious, and no matter how experienced you are as a leader in the gym, under no circumstances are you ready to jump into traditional leading, where you will be placing your own protection and belay anchors. You might have read the books and fondled the gear, and you might have a perfectly sound knowledge of how the traditional lead game works. But you don't have the experience and you haven't developed the feel — such wisdom isn't available from reading or fantasy. You must serve your apprenticeship under an experienced leader before you even consider going it on your own. In fact, most climbers really won't consider you a leader just because you can clip bolts indoors.

What can go wrong on an indoor wall? Relative to the outdoor world, not much. You can buckle or tie-in improperly or your belayer might botch his brake-hand sequence. That's about all you need to worry about.

But how shall I compare this to a summer's day (outdoors)? Let me count the ways:

LOOSE ROCK Not only must you check every foot and handhold when you're on real rock, but you must also expect things to come crashing down from above, even on the most solid-looking cliff.

SHARP EDGES Stretch a climbing

The gym is a great place to meet people, establish indoor partnerships, and make plans for climbs outdoors. It can also be very competitive, with observers keeping a watchful eye.

rope to a couple of hundred pounds between two cars and you can cut it with a butter knife. Consider what a sharp rock edge might do during the huge force of a leader fall.

BAD PROTECTION It rains outdoors. And it snows and freezes and thaws. Metal left in place doesn't respond well to such abuse. Even the best bolts can weaken when subjected to the weather. If you are placing your own gear, figure that some of it is good, much of it suspect, and even the best-looking protection could rip out. Beginning leaders are shocked when that solid-looking placement fails during a fall.

"The Pump Wall" at Point Loma, California. Keep your eyes open and you'll find endless bridge abutments, stone buildings, and retaining walls that will give you a good finger burn. Just make sure you aren't trespassing.

DIFFICULT COMMUNICATION Unless someone has the boom box turned on too high in the gym, you ought not to have too much trouble communicating with your belayer. Outdoors in the wind, over a river or even a stream of traffic, there are times when you can't quite make out what your partner is saying.

CREATURES I've had hornets up my shorts, been startled by a pigeon that brushed my face as it flew from its nest, stuck my fingers into the belly of a bat in a thin crack, surprised a snarling raccoon behind a flake on a high ledge, and had my fixed rope chewed through by rats 2,500 feet up El Capitan. Welcome to nature.

WEATHER On multi-pitch lead climbs, you must be planning your escape from every stance. Indoors, you wonder only if you can do the moves. High on the rock, you must be prepared to beat a hasty retreat when conditions change for the worse.

ROUTE FINDING Don't be disappointed if no one has gone before you and flagged each hold with a color-coded tape. The decisions are yours, and you might find yourself way off the route on territory much more difficult than you anticipated. It's horrifying, but at the same time, it's this kind of uncertainty that makes the adventure of traditional leading so satisfying.

This list isn't intended to scare you away from the glorious outdoors. Let it be a reminder that the transition from plastic to rock is replete with new and serious concerns. Take it slowly.

L E A R N I N G
F R O M
T H E   R O C K

You don't have to be a geologist to enjoy rock climbing, but it helps to understand that the kind of rock you're on plays a major role in determining just how you will climb it. Following are descriptions of three of the major rock types with some specific ideas relating the rock to the techniques it requires.

GRANITE

Granite is a general term that encompasses much of the igneous rock we find. Igneous rock is formed from molten rock, or magma, deep within the earth. As it cools, it crystallizes, and generally, the slower the cooling process, the larger and more developed the crystals. Larger crystals usually mean better friction.

Granite has little in the way of obvious structural patterns like the horizontally bedded sandstone described on page 136. As such, it can seem smooth and holdless. No better examples of this exist than the vast golden walls of Yosemite National Park in California, where sheets of blank rock can stretch for acres without apparent interruption.

The distinctive feature of such granite walls is that when they erode and break down, they do so in sheets parallel to their surface. This process, called *exfoliation*, resembles

Granite climbing is characterized by huge expanses of smooth rock and unrelenting vertical cracks shown here at Yosemite National Park, California.

the peeling of an onion, with layer upon layer flaking away and leaving a fresh surface underneath.

Climbing on granite, therefore, generally involves either moving up cracks formed by exfoliation or simply trying to adhere to the smooth, featureless slabs themselves. There are often very few really positive holds to latch onto, and climbers accustomed to either artificial walls or layered, featured rock like sandstone or limestone find their first visit to a place like Yosemite (or North Carolina or New Hampshire) to be daunting. There's nothing to grab and there's no place to step!

Granite climbers are crack climbers. They live by the hand jam and the layback, two basic maneuvers that allow upward movement on otherwise holdless rock. In both techniques, the climber is holding himself onto the wall by jamming his hands into the crack, but at the same time, he is studying the smooth surface below for any bump or rough spot that will hold his shoe rubber as he pushes his feet against the rock in opposition to the direction he's pulling with his hands. Granite crack climbers know that their climb will probably be a test of endurance, often involving repetitive movements and

self-control. Lose your cool in a lay-back, for instance, and you'll reach too high, the opposition will be lost, and your feet will skid from their tenuous purchase.

The other realm of granite climbing is on its smooth face, usually much less than vertical, but so smooth that the challenges match any presented by steeper, more featured rock. Some friction routes, like North Carolina's Rainy Day Women or New Hampshire's Sliding Board, are among the most popular found anywhere, while others, like Yosemite's 2,000-foot Hall of Mirrors, are so steep and smooth that they have repulsed some of the best climbers.

Granite climbing isn't all the slick stuff of Yosemite legend; some of it is coarse and crystalline enough to allow more traditional face-climbing techniques. In southern California at Joshua Tree National Monument, the rock escaped glacial polishing and thus has had eons of weathering to rough up its surface. The harder crystals resisted erosion while the softer rock eroded, and the result is a very climbable (and nastily sharp-edged) surface. Also renowned for their huge crystals and bizarre face-climbing are the Needles of South Dakota, around and behind the four presidential faces of Mount Rushmore.

SANDSTONE

Sedimentary rock, like sandstone, is formed in the sea, as layer upon layer of sediments are laid down and buried. As the layers are buried deeper and deeper, heat and pressure work to consolidate the grains to form solid rock. Most people associate sandstone with crumbly rock; those people haven't climbed at New River Gorge in West Virginia, or Eldorado Canyon near Boulder, Colorado, or at the Shawangunks in southern New York State. In this popular climbing area, the sandstone grains that make up the white quartzite have been subjected to such compressive pressures that the resulting rock is as hard and compacted as the hardest granite.

Two factors influence the make-up of sedimentary rock: the size and kind of sand grain, and the matrix, or "glue," that holds them together. Think of your days at the beach playing in the waves. If the water was turbulent during the sedimentation, then the individual grains could be quite sizable. The Shawangunks are generally constructed of such pebble-sized "sand," indicating that the shallow sea in which the sediment was deposited was in motion. Around Boston, the "Puddingstone" rock where local climbers have trained for many years has grit the size of base-balls. Try to imagine the conditions necessary for this. At the other end of the grain-size spectrum are the shales and slates, slick indeed.

The glue comes from chemical bonding under huge heat and pressure. Sometimes the grains themselves are hard enough, but they just aren't stuck together very tightly. If the compaction is thorough, however, the glue is so good that when the rock cracks, it does so right through the grains themselves, leaving sheared-off pebbles and grains.

Some of the best climbing in the Eastern United States is in the Sandstone Belt, which runs from Northern Alabama through eastern Tennessee into West Virginia and Kentucky. The routes here are short (seldom exceeding 100 feet) but are awesomely steep. The rock juts out in multi-tiered overhangs, but because of the nature of horizontally-bedded sedimentary rock, the handholds are often flat, sharp, and accommodating.

Such dauntingly steep rock pre-

Mike Freeman demonstrates the finger strength and gymnastic technique required of steep sedimentary rock at New York State's famed Shawangunks.

sents challenges quite different from those found on granite, though similar to the routes set up in climbing gyms. Initially, one would assume that such climbing was the stuff of brute, ape-like strength, or "thuggish" climbing, as one British visitor called it. True, climbing overhanging rock indeed requires strong arms and

Southern sandstone is often overhanging and strenuous, yet no problem for Lynn Hill at New River Gorge, West Virginia.

back muscles. But it requires alertness and technique as well.

Overhanging rock is often laced with good holds, but the problem is reaching and holding onto them. Climbing on such rock requires momentum, almost lunging from one good hold to the next. This is *dynamic* climbing, and it's a long way from the static and controlled styles of the past. When a climber refers to a "dyno," he's describing a long reach that is usually accomplished by grabbing two hands on a hold, running the feet high, then pulling and almost leaping upward. At the maximum height of the move, and just at the moment when the climber would begin to drop, he's weightless, at

ACCESS ISSUES

All recreational-land users run into some conflicts concerning their rights to use a particular property, public or private. Climbers are no different. Here in America, climbing takes place on private, state, and federal lands, and, increasingly, our rights to use those lands are being debated and defined. Using private property, obviously, requires permission of the landowner. Some landowners post their property with specific restrictions; others simply look the other way, willing to let people use

their lands as long as their activities don't ruin the place and only as long as the perceived risk of liability is low. Whatever the case, it's wrong to violate a landowner's wishes as posted on the property.

State and federal land management plans are continually developing. City and state parks and recreational areas vary, and it's essential to find out ahead of time what's legal use and what's not. On the federal level, the Bureau of Land Management and the National Park Service are drawing up new guidelines for the increased climbing use they are

what we call the *deadpoint*, the time when he can let go with one hand and make a controlled stab at the higher hold. Climbers who are good at such dynamic climbing, whose strength is high, and especially those whose timing is precise, can pull dynos of four feet and more between holds. Obviously, you'll be working on dynos in a controlled and safe setting on a top-rope!

Steep, layered rock also allows for some inventive uses of the feet, foremost among them being the *heel-hook*. If you can hook your heel over a sharp hold above your head, you'll have three "hands" pulling for you instead of two. Your hamstring muscles are key here: By pulling upward with your leg as you crank with your arms, you can make a much longer reach than you could otherwise achieve.

Not all sandstone is so clearly banded. Much of the American Southwest is red sandstone, left by eons of erosion as towering monoliths so familiar in cowboy movies and car commercials. Utah, for example, is renowned for its Canyonlands region, with its expanses of dramatic rock split by vertical cracks, somewhat like those found in granite. Interestingly, many of these cracks can be even smoother and more parallel than their granite counterparts, and many such routes aren't conceivable without spring-loaded camming

experiencing. Land owners and governmental agencies have many of the same concerns. They are:

- Risk of liability if someone is injured or killed
- Concerns about environmental impact
- Protection of historical and archaeological sites
- Concerns of overcrowding
- A desire to keep "multi-use" areas from being dominated by a special interest group.

As a climber, you need to do your part to ensure that areas remain open to climbing and that the impact from climbers remains low. The Access Fund leads the way.

Climbers in many areas of the country have earned not only the respect, but also the gratitude of local authorities by involving themselves so responsibly in numerous ways. Volunteer climbers are assisting with peregrine falcon research, training forest rangers and rescue teams, working in search and rescue, and demonstrating in countless other ways that they are responsible users of outdoor resources.

Pocketed limestone, the classic rock of southern France, shows up in a few American climbing areas, such as Wild Iris, in Wyoming.

edges and pockets for your feet. Even as your body becomes horizontal, you can be taking a big part of your weight by "grabbing" and pulling with your toes under the overhang.

LIMESTONE

European climbers, particularly the French, see limestone as the essence of sport climbing. Limestone is often steep and pocketed, offering bizarre and unpredictable linkages of tiny one- and two-finger holds with very little by way of positive footholds.

Limestone is similar to sandstone in that it was formed in water eons ago. But instead of being composed of sand grains, it is made up of the minute shells of marine organisms. It is essentially one big fossil. Countless little guys with names like *radiolaria, miogypsinids, foraminifera,* and many others, donated their tiny calcarious hard parts many years ago to an aggregation of matter that hardened and rose above the sea to form the white limestone cliffs so favored by climbers the world over. We should be grateful. In most limestone, the individual shells are too small to see with the naked eye, but in some formations, you can make out the little swirls and dots of individual organisms.

Footwork on limestone can be especially frustrating: The rock is often quite smooth, and the pockets that might have been useful for a few fingers are too tight for a good shoe

devices for protection.

This Southwestern sandstone is also more suspect; much of it isn't well-consolidated, and on some climbing routes, you can scratch the surface with your fingernails. Yet even with its uncertainty, there is an unparalleled beauty to the surreal landscapes of the desert Southwest where a band of desert rock aficionados somehow maintain sanity while tiptoeing on what the rest of us would call a vertical beach.

Whatever the quality of the rock, don't forget that even on the steepest routes, footwork is the basis of all you do. As you reach high and outward onto those intimidating holds on an overhang, continue to look for

South Dakota's granitic Needles — the same rock into which the four presidents' faces are carved at Mount Rushmore — are both bizarre and enticing. But just don't fall; the protection is meager and the rock coarse and crystalline.

purchase. Typically, limestone climbers want a shoe so soft that they can stick a pointed toe into such pockets, almost as if they were barefoot. Additionally, limestone polishes easily — a boon to the mason, but a curse to the climber. After only a few ascents, a limestone foothold can begin to shine. Scary sometimes when you are used to a gritty and secure surface underfoot.

Rather than breaking up into some kind of pattern, like the horizontal beds of sandstone and the exfoliation slabs of granite, limestone is unpredictable. It is typically dotted with holes called *solution pockets*. Some of these might be big, welcoming, hand-sized "buckets," but often they are little more than single- or double-finger depressions that can do in even the hardiest of tendons. Climbers on limestone must train their fingers carefully; some even tape each finger by wrapping a figure-8 band of narrow athletic tape to support the tendon as it passes over the inside of the joint. Clearly, here is where an open grip is critical to the maintenance of healthy fingers.

Because limestone doesn't crack into patterns like other kinds of rock, there are seldom good natural protection placements for the leader, and most limestone routes are bolt-protected. In southern France, the small

Huge "huecos," scoops and depressions, can make even the steepest terrain relatively easy, as here at Hueco Tanks, Texas.

American wilderness areas.

AND THEN THERE'S...

America is blessed with a wide variety of rock types, well beyond the general categories I've described. There's Smith Rock in Oregon, where a volcanic rock called *welded tuff* juts out from the surrounding landscape, offering almost endless tiny edges and pockets and tempting the world's best climbers out onto terrain that at first seems blank as a chalkboard. There's Devil's Tower in southeastern Wyoming, another volcanic remnant, this one a "plug" left over from an eroded volcano, like a giant tree stump sticking out nearly 800 feet above the prairie. Climbing here takes place on and between the towns near cliffs promote bolting almost as a civic responsibility, and the windows of hardware stores advertise deals on power-drills and other bolting equipment. It's easy to see how the European ethic ran into conflict when it descended upon

giant columns into which the volcanic rock cooled. Devil's Tower climbers are master *stemmers,* able to spread their legs wide to bridge the gap between these unrelenting towers of stone.

There's Hueco Tanks in Texas, where rocks left to the fury of centuries of sandstorms have worn into fantastic shapes, bizarre hollows called *huecos,* creating short strenuous routes in the

An American landmark and a climber's dream: Devil's Tower in northeastern Wyoming, a volcanic "plug" cooled into symmetrical vertical columns. Legend holds that the cracks are the claw marks of a gigantic bear.

southern sunshine, making Hueco Tanks a popular wintering area for America's traveling climbers. And then there are the endless incarnations of *metamorphic* rock, rock that began as one type but which was buried, subjected to tremendous heat and pressure, and twisted into wild formations. Wyoming's Tetons, sec-

tions of Colorado's Rockies, and numerous other smaller crag areas are of metamorphic rock, so varied and unpredictable that it would be futile to try to describe any specific techniques required to climb it.

Whatever the medium, natural rock or indoor plastic, a few principles rule: Be alert and notice all that the surface is offering you. And be creative, adjusting your movements to match. A climber doesn't push himself onto a rock and try to subdue it. He learns from it and adjusts his techniques to it.

The Devil's Tower climber must be loose in the legs to bridge the gaps between the towering columns.

RAPPELLING

You're familiar with the scene: A man bounds boldly down a steep rock face on a thin nylon line. He stops and gazes over the land, chin out, cigarette jutting from clenched teeth. He's a manly guy doing a manly thing. Now erase that picture... forever.

Rappelling is not a daredevil game of risk; it's simply a means to get efficiently down from a high place. Few see it as a sport in itself. Given the choice, we would rather pack away the rope for a leisurely walk back down the trail to the base of the climb.

Simply put, rappelling is the process of sliding down a stationary rope, applying some kind of friction on the rope to check speed and control the descent. The term *rappel* is French. It comes from the verb rappeller, which means "to call back." Rappelling is practical only if the climber can get his rope back when he's down. This is achieved by doubling the rope around or through some anchor, rappelling on both strands, and once on the ground, pulling one strand through to retrieve, or "call back," the rope. A single-strand rappel is possible, but this defeats the original purpose, since the rope remains tied to the top when the rappel is finished.

If the distance to the ground is

Correct rope setup for a figure-8 descender.

THE GEAR

To begin, you'll have to choose a rappel device, some kind of metal gizmo that provides friction on the rope. The first two listed here are by far the most common; the others are essentially tricks to know if for some reason you need to function without the proper gear.

more than one rope length, the climbers must stop along the way, establish new anchors, pull their rope, and begin anew. We call this making "multiple" rappels. It isn't practical to increase the length of a rappel by stringing several ropes together. Passing the knot through the rappel device is a complex procedure, reserved for experts.

The Figure-8 Descender

The figure-8 descender is the most common friction device. (Don't confuse it with the knot of the same name.) The rope passes through as shown (above), and the rappeller controls the rope with his brake hand. The process works just like belaying: the brake hand is crucial, and as it is applied, the friction of rope on metal keeps the descent under control. Some figure-8s have the small ring configured to duplicate a plate-type belay device (pictured on page 82). It's helpful to get multiple functions from single pieces of gear.

The traditional body rappel was popular in the days of stout woolen pants and heavy jackets. It has its disadvantages compared with today's reliable belay devices, but it is worth knowing; in a pinch it can save lives.

The Belay Tube

Another common method is to use a tube-shaped belay device (Black Diamond ATC, Lowe Tuber, Trango Pyramid, HB Sheriff) in its double-rope mode. It may not be as smooth as the classic figure-8, but it is a piece of gear already on your rack, so why not take full advantage of it? It doesn't make sense to carry one unit for belaying and another for rappelling when one item will accomplish both functions. Tube-style rappel/belay devices are the lightest units for the purpose.

ALTERNATIVE METHODS

Other methods work in a pinch. There's the classic "Dulfersitz," where the climber straddles the rope, pulls the rope from behind, up over the head and across the shoulder, painfully achieving the necessary friction by the body alone — no harness, no hardware, (no fun).

Carabiners alone also work for rappelling. The "six-'biner brake" is good, but it's complicated and has lots of moving parts, thus lots of ways it can malfunction. I use it frequently; it allows me to climb without carrying extra gear for descent. Get to know this one exactly, and make sure it's right. Keep it in your bag of tricks for when you drop your friction device.

The Munter hitch

(see "Knots," page 123) also works, but it's best with a large-mouth, pear-shaped carabiner. It twists the ropes and rubs rope on rope as it runs through and over the carabiner. For these reasons, it should be used only as a rare substitute for your regular system.

The GriGri can work for a single rope rappel, yet most rappelling applications use a doubled rope. There's a clever way to rig it for a double rope rappel, but I'll leave that to the instruction manual. Suffice it to say that the GriGri isn't a rappel device, and you'd be better off having other gear available for the job.

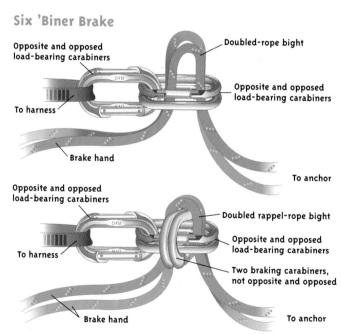

Six 'Biner Brake

Opposite and opposed load-bearing carabiners

Doubled-rope bight

To harness

Opposite and opposed load-bearing carabiners

Brake hand

To anchor

Opposite and opposed load-bearing carabiners

Doubled rappel-rope bight

To harness

Opposite and opposed load-bearing carabiners

Two braking carabiners, not opposite and opposed

Brake hand

To anchor

Carabiners alone can be combined to create a rappel brake. Look closely to make absolutely sure that the two load-bearing pairs of 'biners have opposed gates. The braking carabiners aren't opposed: the rope must run over two solid shafts.

ANCHORING THE ROPE

Most rappels require a full-length, 165-foot rope, and so rather than doubling a single rope (and getting only 80 feet or so), we tie two ropes together and rappel both strands. The second rope can be carried in a pack or dragged by the second. The ideal knot joining the ropes is secure, low-profile (so that it will allow smooth retrieval), and easy to untie after being weighted. The surest is the double-fisherman's, though other options exist. The double figure-8 knot is gaining popularity because it cleverly rides up away from the rock, leaving a smooth rope surface as it passes over the edge during retrieval. Leave at least ten inches of tail, since this one can flip inside out if tied too loosely!

If a rope is to be retrieved, it must run through or over some solid anchor. The simplest is a tree. If the tree is solid and the bark is smooth enough for pulling the rope, then all would be well if it weren't for the damage you inflict on the trunk as you retrieve your rope. To save the tree, use slings and descending rings.

When you come upon an anchor with slings already in place, check to see if they seem new and safe. Don't hesitate to leave your own as a backup. I once leaned back on an old sling anchor and it broke under my

USING ROPES OF DIFFERENT DIAMETERS

If you are going to use a thinner, say 7-mm or 8-mm, rope for your second rappel rope, remember that the two ropes might slide through your rappel device at different rates. This could actually drag your rope through the anchor as you rappel unaware. Two dangers are associated with this: First, one end of the rope could end up shorter than the other as the ropes slip through the anchor. Second, the rope sliding under body weight could melt or saw through a nylon sling anchor. Metal descending rings lessen the second hazard.

body weight. The $2 backup was cheap insurance. Carry a few slings of one-inch tubular webbing tied with a water knot for the very purpose of backing up fixed rappel anchors. Though not as sleek as the pre-sewn thinner slings, they are cheap and easier to tie around trees. Choose earthtone colors, please.

Rappell anchors can be a tangled mess of old slings. Clean them up by removing the ratty ones and adding new slings (earth tone over bright colors) where necessary.

Sometimes you'll see rappel anchors constructed of slings tied around large rocks jammed against each other or wedged in cracks. These can be very solid, but who knows? Just because someone else judged it safe doesn't mean that it is. Remember, anchors aren't fixed by some regulated authority; they might have been set there by someone who knows less than you do. Use your own judgment, and be ready to part with some gear if you have any doubt at all. *A rappel anchor failure simply must not occur.* Look it over carefully — consider ways you might enhance it — and visualize your loved ones. They wouldn't appreciate any thrift here.

The best set-ups use metal *descending rings* so that the rope won't run directly over the slings as it is retrieved. Such nylon-on-nylon rubbing severely weakens the sling — safe for your descent, but damaged for the next party. Doubled metal rings left in place eliminate this problem. In the

Here the rappel ropes have been joined with an overhand figure-8, a knot that rides cleverly up as the rope is pulled over an edge, reducing the chance of getting your rappel rope stuck. *Note: The knot is only secure if it has at least ten inches of tail.* Note also that there are two separate slings, not just one long one.

with drilled anchor bolts. Never use just one, and make sure that they share the load. (Remember the discussion of equalized anchors in chapter 5, page 79). Make sure that your rappel rope is connected to both anchors so that if one fails, you are still tied into the other one. It's possible to inadvertently loop the rope over the anchors in a way that will be disastrous if one goes.

A prusik knot (see chapter 7, page 123) acts as a backup for the rappel, safeguarding the climber if his brake hand slips or if the descender comes unclipped. The upper hand keeps the prusik cord from jamming.

As always, make the decision carefully as to how secure an anchor is. With bolts, you have no way of knowing except than by visually inspecting them. (Don't tap them with a hammer!) Pitons are notoriously unpredictable. They may have been sound when placed, but they steadily loosen as the rock weathers and the metal rusts.

absence of the rings, leave one of your slings a little shorter than the rest. This will put the stress of the rappel and the abrasion of the retrieval on this one sling, saving the others as backups if the primary one fails.

Increasingly, local climbers are setting up permanent rappel anchors

THE PROCESS

Find a body position that feels comfortable — beginners are typically reluctant to lean back far enough to keep their feet securely on the rock. Recall the concept of opposition from chapter 3, "Movement": The harder you lean back, the more your feet will stick to the rock. Keep the legs about a shoulders-width apart. You can turn slightly to the side to look downward, keeping an eye on the terrain below instead of blindly backing into the unknown. Resist using footholds or ledges. They'll only cause you trouble as you unweight the rope, making it difficult for you to get back into position.

On low-angled rock, rappelling will feel more like walking backwards. Surprisingly, vertical rock is easier because it allows you to sit comfortably back in your harness. The position here is akin to that of sitting in an easy chair with your feet up on the coffee table. Overhanging rock may seem daunting, but it presents no real problems. We call this a "free" rappel, and your first such

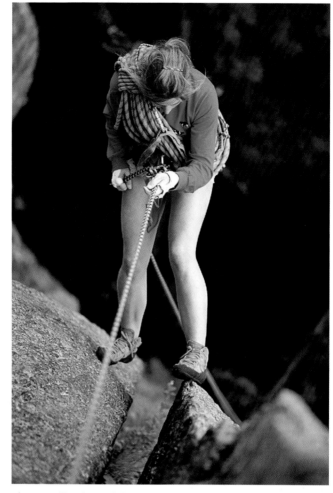

When rappelling, keep a balanced stance, feet about shoulders'-width apart and eyes down on the terrain and footing below.

experiences will be etched into your memory for a long time. As your feet leave the rock, try not to push off to the side and start yourself spinning. But if you do, don't worry. Regardless of how you flail your legs to counter the spin, you'll just keep twisting. Instead of fighting it, enjoy the 360-degree views. (But remember to untwist the rope before you try to retrieve it.)

Backing Up Your Rappel Device

Rappelling is one of the easiest — and most dangerous — elements of climbing. Perhaps that dicotomy is no coincidence. The process is so simple that climbers are lulled into a sense of false security, especially after having just done a difficult climb. But a lot can go wrong: The gear might be set up improperly, the brake hand might slip, the anchors could fail, the rope could abrade on a sharp edge, the rope might not reach the ground, rocks could be dislodged from above. All of these things happen to climbers, yet all are preventable.

It is vital to use some kind of backup when rappelling. It's just too casual to put all of your faith in your brake hand alone. My friend Katie, whose braking arm was smashed by a falling rock and who fell the final 20 feet to the ground, is quick to remind me of just how important the backup system is.

The beginner learns to rappel with a separate rope as a belay. If you are showing someone how to do it, it's irresponsible not to provide this separate backup rope. Once the rappeller is proficient — on all kinds of terrain, low-angled to overhanging — he can go it alone, provided some *other* mechanism is in the place of the belay.

The prusik knot, or one of its variations, is really useful here. The rappeller holds the loose prusik cord in his guide hand; if he lets go with his brake hand, the prusik grabs and averts catastrophe (see photograph on page 150). This setup is the most common. Look at it closely to see how the prusik is attached independent of the rappel gear. The system does, however, create a problem if the prusik jams unexpectedly, especially on overhanging rock. I know an instructor who got quite a lecture from a justifiably angry client who had gotten hung up on the overhanging summit rappel of the Grand Teton in bad weather and who had to cut herself free with a knife. It seems that he had shown her how to set up the prusik backup but had neglected to explain how to get out of it. If you are going to use a prusik in this configuration above the rappel device, *make sure you can free it.* The easiest method is this:

1 Clip a sling to the prusik sling.
2 Step one foot into the sling and stand. (This is strenuous and awkward.)
3 As you stand, pull the brake rope

The spidered rappel. The belay device is on a full-length sling girth hitched onto the harness. The prusik knot backup is connected separately for true redundancy. Make sure the prusik isn't so long as to reach the belay device when loaded. This would render it ineffective.

take your foot out of the sling, loosen the jammed prusik, and continue.

You must be carrying another sling and carabiner to do this, but under no circumstances should you be making a rappel without some extra slings and 'biners available to solve whatever problem presents itself. Practice this one from a low branch of a tree or in another controlled setting.

A Better Method

A better, and admittedly unconventional, rappel is offered at left. Your friends might think it strange at first; even your instructor might not have seen it. But it's as foolproof as any, and it eliminates all the fussing a prusik could cause.

This method depends on an extended rappel device, "spidered" out on a girth-hitched sling (or two, if you wish to double it). The slings aren't clipped onto the harness; they are actually threaded through with a full girth hitch. The prusik is attached to the harness below the braking device, where it is easily tended and where it won't get stuck. Make sure that the prusik is adjusted short enough so that it doesn't reach your rappel device. This would cancel it out as a backup since the prusik wouldn't be allowed to tighten on the rope. (To shorten a prusik, simply tie one or two overhand knots onto the cord.) The advantages of this

upward through the rappel device and hold it locked off.

🔾 Sit back onto the rappel device,

text continued on page 156

CLIMBING THE ROPE

Sometimes an unforeseen problem arises that requires climbing the rope itself. This will occur when the ropes are jammed and won't pull cleanly after a rappel. If all methods of pulling and flipping and tugging the ropes fail, then it's necessary for one of the climbers to ascend the ropes to ascertain and fix the problem. It's no fun, but you've got no other choice.

The method is clumsy at first, and you should practice it in a controlled setting (say, from the branch of a tree in your yard or at the climbing gym, with the consent of the management) until it is *fully* comfortable. Many climbers say they know how to do it. Sure, they've seen the diagrams countless times, but most of these climbers would be hard-pressed to perform it in the real situation.

Ascending a rope is also called prusiking, named for the knot. (The prusik knot is described on page 123. If you must use webbing instead of cord, use the kleimheist, page 124). The climber uses two separate cords prusiked onto the rope, and by sliding these upwards, he can ascend the rope. Sound easy? It's not.

There are several variations of the technique that I'll describe. Cavers and big-wall climbers have really honed this into an art form. But I'm going to simplify this technique so it will meet the needs of the occasional user who is in a jam.

To rig the set-up, start by wrapping a prusik cord around the ropes (both of them) and clipping it with doubled, opposed-gate carabiners to a half-hitched sling from your harness. A girth-hitched sling might be OK for taller climbers, but getting the length just right saves a lot of energy. Experiment with this and learn what length works for you. Ideally, the prusik knot, when pushed up to its maximum height on the ropes, will be at about your elbow as you extend your arm (Figure 1). If the cord is too short, you won't get full extension on each push; if it is too long, you'll have a real battle trying to keep the weight off your arms and onto your harness where it belongs.

The second cord is prusiked underneath and slung as shown. The higher knot is for sitting, and the lower knot is your stirrup for pushing with your leg.

Begin by getting the stretch out of the rope, stepping hard into the lower knot while pushing the upper one higher and higher up the ropes. Once the stretch is out and you can weight the ropes, just sit back into your harness and hang from the ropes (Figure 2). Relax. Don't try to muscle it. Loosen the lower prusik, slide it up the rope, grab the rope with one hand for balance, and stand (Figure 3). Loosen the upper knot with a quick

twist ("breaking" the knot as shown) and slide it upward until you feel the sling come tight on your harness. Then sit back, relax, and hang your arms for a rest (Figure 4). This strenuous part should be short and efficient. If your arms tire as you climb, you aren't being economical with your moves. Practice. Practice. Practice.

Repeat the process until you get to the top of the rope, switching feet every so often if you find your legs tiring.

You're on your way up the dangling lines and will have the problem solved in no time at all. But I hope that you've already noticed something missing: the backup system. All through this book you've gotten the same lec-

continued on page 156

CLIMBING THE ROPE
continued from page 155

ture, and you're going to get it again. Never trust your life to a single piece of gear unless you have no other choice. And in the case of prusiking, you have two good options, both of which should always be in place. These options are:

1. Connect a sling to the lower prusik knot as an unweighted backup. This way you'll at least be into two separate systems.

2. Every 20 feet or so, tie an overhand knot in the two ropes and clip them into your harness with a locking carabiner. If the prusiks fail, you won't go to the ground. Remember to keep each knot tied until the next one is in place. Don't leave yourself vulnerable for a moment.

text continued from page 153

system are several:

❶ The prusik can't jam or break because it takes only a fraction of your weight, and it remains right in easy range for either hand to tend.

❷ You now have *two* hands as brake hands, so the backup is built in.

❸ You won't get hair or chin strap or anything else caught in your rappel device — a real danger with the conventional method.

❹ You can let go at any time. The knot will hold, and you can release it at will — a real plus if you have to do something (clean gear from the route, for example) on your way down. If you need to hang to do any extended work, tie a backup knot linking the rappel rope to your harness just in case.

❺ When you get to the next rappel anchor, you can unclip the rappel carabiner from your device and right into the anchor while keeping your prusik knot in place. This way you are *always* connected during the transition. Likewise, when it's time to rappel, you can put your prusik on before detaching yourself and setting up your rappel device. Never stand near the edge without being connected to something. Make sure that you are clipped to the anchors until you have fully checked your rappel setup and its backup system.

RETRIEVING THE ROPE

Once on the ground or ledge, you must pull one strand of rope in order to get it back. (Did you remember on which side of the anchor rings you left the knot that joined your two ropes? I always identify the strand to my partner with something like "Pull blue" before I start. Saying this out loud and getting confirmation from the other climber ensures that you'll pull the right end and avert the real mess that could occur if you jam the knot into the anchor slings.)

Make sure that the ropes aren't tangled. The last rappeller has the additional responsibility of seeing that the ropes aren't jammed and will pull cleanly. One trick is to have the first climber give a trial tug from below before the second heads down. The second can then fix any potential jams by extending the anchor slings or moving the ropes to a better spot as they pass over the edge. Such a test will save you time over the long run.

If the rope doesn't pull, try the slingshot trick: Each of you will pull

CHECK LIST

- Regard rappelling seriously and cover yourself at all times.
- Stay far from the edge or safely anchored as you are rigging your gear.
- Use a belay or some other kind of backup system.
- Tie a large knot onto the end of each strand of rope so that it would be impossible to rappel off the end of the rope. This unthinkable event has unfortunately happened many times.
- Know how to ascend a free-hanging rope; you might need to go up to free it if it can't be retrieved, or you might have misjudged the distance to the ledge below.
- Check to make sure no clothing that could get caught is hanging above the rappel device. Tuck in shirts, tie back hair, tuck back chin-strap. *Anything* could get dragged into the system. (I've got a harrowing and true story on this topic, but it's too uncomfortable to recount. Your imagination will suffice.)
- Double-check your anchors and never take old slings for granted: Be ready to leave your own gear.
- Don't bounce or swing back and forth while rappelling. It will only stress the anchors and abrade the rope.
- Don't go too fast. Speed causes heat, and heat makes nylon unhappy.
- Once on the ground or ledge below, take shelter from rock fall that is likely when the next rappeller is on the rope or later when you are retrieving the rope and pulling it over the debris on the ledge above.

an end of rope as hard as you can. Once big loads are exerted on the two ropes, release the one you aren't planning to pull. The sharp upward snap is sometimes enough to free the jam above.

If you are in any kind of dangerous terrain, stay tied to the anchors. Otherwise, you'll be in for an unhappy surprise when the rope suddenly unjams.

Rappelling might seem easy, but it can be dangerous if you skip any of the safeguards.

T R A I N I N G

Top climbers are fanatic trainers. Endless sessions in the gym and an obsession with body fat seem to dominate their lives. As a recreational climber, however, you can get fit and still have a life at the same time. You may choose to avoid weight-training altogether, gaining the requisite strength for your climbing ambitions from simply spending time on the rock or the wall. However, if you decide to pursue a training regimen, the rewards are clear: the stronger you get, the better you'll climb and the more likely you'll avoid chronic injuries.

The best way to initiate a training program for climbing is to go to the gym or the crag and climb until you can climb no more. Which muscles are tired? Where is the pain? Answer these questions, and you'll know what to work on.

Weight-lifters know that there are two elements to strength training: power and endurance. Both play key roles in rock climbing, but as you start, you'll want to concentrate on endurance. The fundamental challenge on most climbs is performing when your muscles are fatigued. Endurance-training also helps you resist injury by building muscles rather than tearing down ligaments and tendons, which take much longer to strengthen. You'll need to be patient before pushing them to the limit.

The body-builder may seek powerful symmetry as he sculpts his muscle groups, but the climber wants strength without the bulk and weight. The idealized climber has fingers like stubby sausages, forearms like Popeye, lats like a flying squirrel, and legs like a starved chicken. Realistically, most accomplished climbers are just plain fit, neither scrawny like the marathoner nor beefy like the linebacker.

Any training that fatigues the climbing muscles is good. As you begin working out with weights, keep the weight low and the repetitions high. The pull-down machine at the gym is good. Set a comfortable weight, grab the bar with your fingers and an open grip, and do as many pulls as you can, bringing the bar down as low as possible each time. You are on track when your forearms burn and your back and shoulders are engaged. Also good for the fingers is rolling a weight bar in your hands. Again, start with a low weight but roll until there's fire in your forearms. Here is where the progress is made.

Most people think pull-ups must be the best exercise. They're OK, but there are better ways to do the routine. Place a chair or bench under and a few feet back from the bar. Keep your feet on the chair as you work out. Because the chair is back

from under the bar, you'll be forced to work your shoulders and back, much as you would on overhanging rock. At first, the "cheater" pull-ups will seem ridiculously easy. Then the burn will kick in, first in your forearms, and then in your legs as you frantically try to transfer the weight to whichever part of your body is least tired. Such a routine approximates the struggle up a moderate but unrelenting climb. Remember, it's not always the hard part of a route that will get you. It's often the challenge of hanging in there on the less difficult terrain when your reserves are draining.

Despite all the good work you can do with weights, nothing beats a climbing wall for getting you in shape. It seems that the burn you get while trying to complete a hard route or doing laps on a familiar climb is deeper and more effective than anything you are willing to do to yourself with weights. If you do choose to use climbing as a strength trainer, consider three principles:

❶ Never leave a top-rope hanging with no one on it. While your friends are jawboning about this route or that, ask for a belay and do another lap.

❷ Don't leave the gym or the crag without your forearms bulging and your fingers useless.

❸ And most important, REST. Muscles aren't built when you are tearing them down. The growth happens when they are left alone to recover and grow.

WARMING UP

Climbing can put unexpected stresses on the body, both because of the unusual positions you'll find and because, once the competitive instinct kicks in, you won't want to back off without giving a move your maximum effort. Don't even consider a hard climb until you are warmed up and stretched.

Warm-up includes both a cardio-vascular and a muscular component. A light jog is good to get your systems moving and your muscle groups warm. Even a few pull-ups will help before you begin the real climbing. Muscles are looser and stronger after they've gotten a rigorous workout.

Stretching is also vital for climbing well and keeping injury free. Fingers and forearms, shoulder joints and back muscles need to be loosened. Also, the high step and wide stem required of rock climbers demand that you stretch your groin, quads, and hamstrings. Finally, get the calf muscles stretched, both for efficient climbing and to reduce the trembling feet that can be associated with strenuous footwork.

INJURIES

Every sport has its injuries. Tennis elbows, football knees, even typists' wrists — chronic joint-specific ailments seem to typify many activities. Climbing is no exception. But if you ease into it gradually, letting the muscles and tendons adjust to the new demands of climbing, you can reduce the incidence and severity of injury. Most climbing pain comes from simple overuse of a joint or muscle. Such overuse is usually the result of trying too hard too many times on the same climbing move. When you do this, you subject your body to an unusual strain over and over again, and the result will be a pulled muscle, a swollen joint, or the climber's curse — tendinitis. Fingers, elbows, and shoulders are the body parts that bear the most load during a hard climb and are consequently most likely to be injured.

Fingers

Finger injuries are usually caused by either unnatural twisting (as in jamming a vertical finger-sized crack) or using a "crimp" grip, which bends the first joint in the finger backwards, stressing the joint. Strong, well-trained hands can take such exertion in occasional and reasonable doses, but repeated stresses or stress applied to untrained fingers can quickly become a problem.

To reduce the likelihood of such finger injuries, be sure to warm up sufficiently before climbing. Gentle stretching is the best way to start. Squeezing a hand exerciser or even a tennis ball as part of your warm-up routine will also help quite a bit. So will beginning your climbing day with a couple of "warm-up routes," climbs well within your ability that will allow the whole body to become

The crimp grip puts unnatural stresses on the finger joints. Use the open grip whenever possible to keep stress to a minimum.

stretched, warm, and ready. Once you are in action, try to use an open grip as much as possible, saving the stressful crimp only for extreme situations. And be patient if you can't succeed on a route first day. It's better to come back rested than to blow your whole season by stubbornly trying until you are hurt.

Elbows

Elbow problems have afflicted many of the best climbers, and some have had their careers interrupted or even ended by severe tendinitis. The elbow is under the most stress when a climber pulls a hold low into his chest. Picture someone doing a pull-up: He'll probably stop when his hands reach about the level of his chin, a position that most healthy elbows can handle. Pulling down

lower than this (impossible for many of us anyway) begins to do nasty things to the elbow joint. Modern gym routes, overhanging with good holds for hands and feet, are especially dangerous in that they allow even weaker climbers to do radically low pulls.

Shoulders

Shoulder injuries seem to be of two types. Extended "hangs" on straight arms with unflexed shoulders can loosen and endanger the shoulder joint. If you plan to train using finger hangs as part of your routine, make sure your arms are slightly flexed so that muscle, not joint, takes the brunt of your weight. Another stressful movement for your shoulders is weighting the joint in an unusual position, such as you might encounter when you reach to the side to grab a hold. Your shoulders are accustomed to exertion in a typical pull-up position. But in the stress of a climb, you might inadvertently ask your shoulder joint to perform when it's out of position. Several climbers have experienced shoulder separations during a climb — not only painful, but potentially disastrous.

In addition to sensible training of the specific climbing muscles, make sure that you also work on the "antagonist" muscles as well. This is especially applicable to the fickle shoulder joint. In other words, you can stabilize and strengthen the joint by making sure that the whole joint is well-trained. In the case of the shoulder joint, you should also include "push" exercises like push-ups and military presses.

Some basic principles to keep in mind to avoid injuries are:

❶ Think about how your joints are designed and try to work within their natural range.

❷ Warm up and stretch joints and muscles before putting them to task on a climb.

Difficult routes often require long reaches, which in turn require well-toned and stretched joints and muscles. Nevertheless, this climber's lower (right) elbow won't be especially happy about such abuse.

❸ Stay hydrated.

❹ Avoid overuse, and quit before that first twinge, which signals an injury.

Getting Well

My own worst climbing injury occurred from trying to remove a stubborn ice hammer stuck in soft ice. It was the first ice climb of the year (no, I didn't warm up). The recalcitrant tool was off to the side, and for about ten minutes, I twisted and pried. It was only after I had called it a few choice names that it finally wriggled free. I felt no pain and finished the climb easily. Next day, my forearm was tender, and by evening it actually squeaked when I moved. My friends could hear it across the room. If I were a driven climber, I would have been in trouble, but I'm not. I'm a wimp, and I immediately visited my doctor (also a climber) who explained tendinitis, put me in a splint, and gave me strict instructions about rest and icing. In a little more than a week, I was back in business. Ever since then, when I feel the first hint of a strain, I back off, sometimes even splinting a finger, not because it's badly injured, but because I know that it needs a rest and that I don't want to go through what far too many of my friends have suffered.

During injury, there are countless ways to stay active and even in shape. Get on your bike. Increase your jogging miles. Stretch. Work those muscles that aren't injured. *But don't go back to the rock and make it any worse.* Any climber who has battled tendinitis will tell you this. Learn from his mistakes.

PREPARING
FOR
TROUBLE

If you keep your head about you and climb conservatively and safely, you'll reduce the chances that something will go wrong and someone will be hurt. Even so, you should approach every climb and every climbing situation *as though* something is going to happen. This will force you to be ready for it and it will greatly facilitate whatever response you have to make.

Most basic is that you approach all climbing *defensively*. Set up your ropes and anchor systems with the presumption that something might fail. Think ahead of time about what backups you should integrate into your system to cover such a mishap.

Simple common sense is essential here. Stay tied in any time you are in hazardous terrain. Increasingly, accidents are occurring as people walk in and around climbing areas; they let down their guard when they aren't actually climbing, exposing themselves to rockfall from above or slipping unroped on hazardous terrain.

View other climbers as dangerous. (I know, they are probably nice people. Go ahead, talk to them. But in your mind, believe that they are paid assassins, plotting to drop a rock on you as soon as you walk into their sights.) Don't linger beneath groups on top of a cliff. Stay sheltered from rock fall whenever pos-

Steve Levin moving up the *King of Swords* route at Colorado's remote Diamond on Long's Peak. In such remote settings, climbers are on their own; quick rescue is impossible and all precautions must be taken.

another party to his left. Below, a novice woman was struggling with a 5.9 as her top-rope came flying down from above and landed on her head! Unthinkable, and if I hadn't seen it for myself, I wouldn't believe anyone could be so stupid. Moral — they are all out to get you. Be alert.

Basic also to defensive climbing is a good first aid kit. Keep one available in all situations. At a top-rope area, you can keep it in your pack. But when you get off the ground on multi-pitch terrain, what are you going to do if someone gets injured? At the very least, you should have a small knife and some athletic tape. With creative use of a T-shirt and webbing, you may be able to fashion an effective bandage or splint.

sible. Make sure that you and others use names when communicating to each other. I once saw someone unclip and drop an anchored top-rope from a 75-foot cliff top, completely unaware that it wasn't his rope that he'd detached but that of

Better still, carry your first aid gear in a small pack. Such a pack can be worn by the second and can contain more complete medical gear. In addition to the knife and tape, you should include latex gloves, a triangle bandage, gauze, tweezers, a small flashlight (with extra bulb and batteries), a thin space-blanket, and a pencil and paper for emergency notes. All can fit easily into a fanny pack, leaving room for water and snacks.

On any route where there is the slightest possibility of being caught in deteriorating weather or where you just might be forced to spend the night, you should carry at least the minimum gear to protect yourself. Include rainwear, and dress sensibly in pile-type clothes that retain their warmth when wet. Heed my rescue friend's grim adage: "The best-dressed corpses wear cotton."

The old-time climbers used to scoff at carrying bivouac gear, saying that "If you carry overnight gear, you'll end up needing it." Yet even if you aren't taking full bivouac gear, there is some sensible middle ground. When you are stuck in the rain, even only a pitch or two from the ground, it is essential that you can either get down quickly or function in the cold. As you get soaked and chilled, you'll be increasingly unable to perform, shivering and fumbling with even basic rope-handling. A pile jacket and thin raincoat might not be sufficient for a full-conditions bivy, but they'd make all the

difference as you face the unexpected change in weather.

When all goes well, you are back by happy hour boasting of your adventure. But one stuck rope, one route-finding error, one slight injury, and you are groping about in the dark. Do not go high without your flashlight or headlamp. Friends recently described making multiple rappels in the dark. There was a hint of irony as they described the beautiful night, and how their rappel devices were *probably* set up right.

A SELF-RESCUE PRIMER

OK. You've done everything right and something still happens. Someone dislocates a shoulder, or takes a lead fall breaking his leg, or a rock crashes into someone from above. These things can and do happen, and when they do, the climber partners must respond quickly and effectively.

■

NOTE: What you'll see here are the beginnings of some fairly sophisticated techniques. Although they will seem bewildering to the beginner, it is every climber's responsibility to continue to learn. Don't get bogged down in this section right away. Use it as a resource that will make more and more sense as you gain proficiency in the basics. Remember, this book isn't meant to replace experience or professional instruction, but to accompany and stimulate you as you learn. I suspect that as you get into the sport, the tricks that follow will intrigue you and you'll want to know more. Professional guide services offer excellent "self-rescue" courses. Certainly, as you become an independent climber venturing onto higher and more committing terrain, it is incumbent upon you to know how to get yourself and your partner out of a jam. And so when the rest of the game begins to make some sense and you are ready to get to work practicing in a controlled and safe setting, read on.

Effective response initially means taking stock of the situation. Calm down. Take a few deep breaths. And *know* that you will rise to the occasion and perform well. Panic certainly isn't going to be of any use here. Instead, it's time to rely on those fundamental rescue options

that you have practiced so many times that they are fully understood and comfortable to perform.

I won't go into advanced or complicated rescue here. An introductory text just isn't the place for such instruction. Instead, I'll offer some basic "tools" of rescue, maneuvers and tricks that are the foundation of more advanced technique, and operations that I hope will pique your interest to know more. The more you practice these in a controlled setting, and the more you discuss such contingencies with your partners, the more ready you'll be to face the awful things that can happen out there.

As you become proficient at self-rescue, you'll come to rely on the following techniques:

Locking off Your Belay Device

In almost every emergency involving climbing, the first thing a belayer must do is lock off his belay device. This involves locking off the rope so that the load is transferred to the anchor and the belayer can free his hands to function. Not only does this allow the belayer to begin some kind of rescue procedure, but more basically, it gives him a chance to let go and to relax. Admittedly, even the most practiced climbers will find an emergency frightening, and when you are squeezing the juice out of the belay rope, you can't think clearly or calmly. Your initial task, then, is to free your hands, assess the situation, and come up with a plan. You aren't sitting next to a pay phone, and so you can't expect the 911 boys to be arriving in a minute or two as you've seen on TV. It's your responsibility to respond.

The way you lock off the rope depends mainly on what type of belay you are using. If you are belaying with the traditional hip belay (but why were you doing so in

LIGHTNING

Lightning kills over 100 people every year in the United States, and the most vulnerable are those caught unexpectedly in high or open places: Read "climbers." Though some areas of the country are especially prone to lightning storms (Colorado's Front Range, for example), no place is immune.

Consider lightning as a possibility every time you prepare to go up, and plan ahead what you are going to do. First, get low. Staying high on an exposed ridge needlessly makes you a target, and it's far better to have backed off a route and see blue sky above than to ignore the rumblings and find your hair standing on end.

Prudent planning includes:
- Having an up-to-date local weather forecast before you go up.
- Knowing in advance every possible quick escape or rappel route.
- Choosing routes that face the approaching weather; if the storm moves over from behind the cliff, you'll be caught by surprise.
- Getting an early start and trying to be down before the typical period of afternoon electrical activity.

If you do find yourself in an electrical storm:
- Stay away from mouth of a cave or overhang where a jolt could jump from the floor to the roof as it makes its connection.
- Stay low and don't lean against the cliff, one potential path of electric current.
- Stay away from bodies of water or tall objects, like trees. It's better to be in a dense thicket.

the first place?), you must wrap the brake side of the rope several times around your thigh in order to free your hands. This can be awkward if your stance and anchor aren't solid. If, on the other hand, you are using a GriGri, then it is already locked off once the load has been applied.

If you are using some kind of belay plate or tube device, follow the steps as illustrated in Figures 1–3 (below). Once the doubled rope is tied onto the climbing rope, the belay is locked fast. Some texts will show a different and more complicated method for this, but for the recreational climber who wants to function using basic tools and techniques, the overhand lock-off works just fine. It's simple and secure, and it's releasable after it's been loaded. Additionally, it leaves you a loop that can be clipped off with a carabiner in order to add to its security. I tell my students to practice locking off the rope every time they lower someone just so that the maneuver

ESCAPING THE BELAY

To tie-off you must lock off the belay device. 1) Pull a long bight of rope through your belay carabiner. 2) Make sure you have 3 feet of rope to work with. 3) Tie an overhand knot around the climbing rope right over your belay device. 4) Your hands are free. If you also need to get yourself free from the belay, wrap a prusik or kleimheist around the rope. 5) Clip the prusik to the belay either with a sling or with the climbing rope (as shown). 6) Once you release the locked-off belay device, the climber's weight will transfer to the prusik. Don't rely on this alone: Clove-hitch the brake rope to the anchor before you take yourself out of the system.

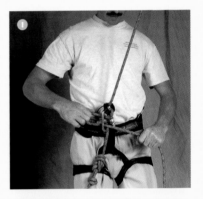

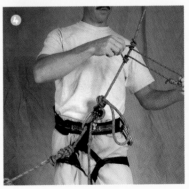

will become a habit.

Obviously, as you practice this one, you'll want to do so only when your partner is safely only a few feet from the ground. And when you release the knot and resume lowering, make sure you have the rope securely belayed as you do. There should be no gaps in your sequence that make the lowering climber vulnerable.

Escaping the Belay
Some rescue scenarios will require

you to either run for help or somehow reach your injured partner. Here is where you must know how to "escape the belay." To do so, you must have an anchor good for an upward pull (another good reason to set up carefully *before* you start the climb). Once you have locked off the belay device and can function with both hands, you must wrap a prusik knot onto the rope and attach it to the anchor. Once this is set, you can gently release the locked-off rope and ease the load onto the anchored prusik, watching it

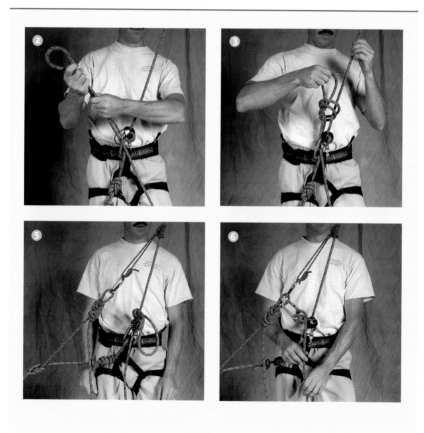

carefully to make sure that the prusik catches and holds. Once this is effected, you are no longer in the system and are free to untie and leave, but not until you have tied off some kind of backup knot in case the prusik slips. It isn't prudent to leave a climber attached only to a 6- or 7-mm cord and friction knot.

Now you are free. What are you going to do? Do you have a knife? Perhaps you'll need to cut a section of the remaining rope to get down or to reach the climber from above if such an extreme measure were your best option. Can you ascend the rope with prusiks (see "Climbing the Rope," page 154)? Can you safely leave the scene to get help? Admittedly, none of these options is easy or ideal, but having the freedom to exercise them sure beats just hanging on to the belay and hoping someone arrives.

Tandem Rappelling

By extending the rappel from a doubled sling (as described and shown on page 153), you are also in a good position to perform a dual rescue rappel. Set up as you would for a *spidered rappel*, with the prusik knot below as a backup. Clip your injured partner right into your locking carabiner, and hold his weight away from the wall by pushing off with your legs. The climber can hang free sideways to you as you control the friction of the rappel. Such a maneuver requires that the climber be at least conscious and somewhat cooperative.

This technique is much like the big-wall climbers' method of rappelling with a heavy haul-bag. Clipping the bag to the rappel carabiner instead of trying to wear it like a backpack transfers the load to the rappel device and makes for a much easier ride. Wall climbers straddling the dangling bag call it "riding the pig," but you should be more respectful of your partner as you describe your heroics following your epic rescue.

These operations are only the most basic of self-rescue. I hope that as you become a climber, you'll take the initiative to learn more from reading more detailed rescue texts and by taking a rescue course from a professional. As the numbers using our mountain areas increase, it's good to know that many of the newcomers are taking with them a responsible desire to learn as much as they can to make sure that their climbs are safe.

GOING
FURTHER

The skills you've learned will be a foundation upon which to build throughout a long and safe climbing career. Maybe you'll be content to stay in the gym and continue to enjoy the controlled challenges of sport climbing. Here you can choose to aim for some routes that are, for the moment, just out of your reach, and you can train specifically toward the day when they might be attainable. You might even choose to sign up for one of the competitions offered at the local gym. Who knows where such events might lead you?

Or maybe your goals are loftier.

Some of your best climbing experiences may be found on long, multi-pitch rock routes, climbs that might not be as extreme as those you've been working on in the lowlands, but ones that offer the heightened satisfaction of keeping gear organized, holding the chatter to a minimum, being quick in transition at belays, and moving efficiently over the high terrain. Such long routes will focus you on a single goal, and you'll find that one ten-pitch route is much more rewarding than ten single-pitch climbs.

You may be comfortable with 5.10 climbing on the short crags close to home, but when you head for the hills, tone down your numerical ambitions and choose instead climbs

Above: The Trango Tower in northeastern Pakistan is one of the world's greatest climbing challenges.
Right: No room service here. El Capitan climbers adjust to days and nights on end on the wall.

of lower grades. The length, not the technical difficulty, will be the central challenge. Such a climb requires good planning: choosing gear, planning for the unplanned bivouac, learning about the approach and the descent, checking route descriptions and weather forecasts, and considering how you are going to make a fast escape if conditions change. You'll be up well before the sun — perhaps from a high camp near the base of the route — and you'll be moving fast. Yet no matter how quick you think you are, the hours will slip by and those darkening cumulus clouds building nearby are reminders to get that rappel underway and head safely down where you can relax for the first time in a long day.

You might expect such multi-pitch routes to be limited to the Western mountain states, but that isn't the case. In the Southeast, the longest routes are on North Carolina Granite: Looking Glass Rock and Stone Mountain are in the moderate realm, while the awesome and overhanging Whitesides Mountain is reserved for only the most experienced climbers. Up north, New Hampshire's Cannon Mountain offers climbs nearing 1,000 feet, and nearby Cathedral and Whitehorse Ledges stand 500 or so feet above the valley floor. In the Adirondacks of New York State, there's Poke-O-Moonshine (500 feet) and the wild and remote Wallface, where the three-hour approach is followed by

Wyoming's Tetons and Wind River Range, Colorado's Rocky Mountain National Park, California's High Sierra all offer the best of climbing with endless views and awesome exposure.

You've moved now from cragging to mountaineering, and your skills and judgments will be tested much more rigorously. Route-finding, loose rock, and various other uncertainties have become part of the game, and the world has expanded far

Lynn Hill competing at Berkeley, California. Hill is one of the world's top climbers, male or female. She has free-climbed El Capitan and dominated the world competition scene.

routes of up to eight pitches long. Quebec has some of the highest Eastern cliffs of all, with Cap Trinite towering more than 800 feet high over the Saguenay River.

Some of the best long-route climbing anywhere can be found on the "alpine rock" in the West.

beyond the difficulty of a single move, such as you remember from your first rock climb.

Maybe your aspirations will lead to big-wall fantasies and the vast golden acres of Yosemite. Such climbing requires proficiency in aid climbing and thorough understanding of gear use and rope management. Big-wall climbing is akin to vertical engineering: pendulums and pulleys, hooking fragile edges and hauling big loads, with rest finally found on a fragile skin of nylon stretched across the frame of your "port-a-ledge." It's been said that multi-day big-wall climbing is 10 percent fun and 90 percent work — and it will seem so when you're up there, struggling to heft a 100-pound bag to your hanging belay and counting the days until you top out. Perhaps. But few rock-climbing experiences can match the intensity of focus you'll find when you are days up a smooth wall like Half Dome or El Capitan.

A hanging bivouac high on Half Dome at Yosemite.

Perhaps the ultimate rock-climbing game is to combine all the skill areas, to take the big-wall approach into the high and remote alpine ranges. Alaska and Baffin Island, the Canadian Rockies and Greenland — places like these have scores of unclimbed and even unnamed walls that would test even the best climbers. The approaches are hard, and the remoteness is especially acute when you look down from your hanging bivouac not at the lights of town, but at a lonely tent among the boulders.

Even bigger and more sheer are the rock walls of Patagonia on the harsh southern tip of South America. Cerro Torre and Fitzroy are two of the mythical towers that have drawn many but rewarded few. And the

A climber's-eye view of the Himalayas from the southwest ridge of Ama Dablam (mother's charm box) not far from Mount Everest. There are no limits to where the sport can take you.

biggest of them all are in the high Himalayas: the great rock faces of Nepal and Pakistan, where even El Capitan would be dwarfed by the giant gray faces.

Your journey will probably never end. Maybe work and family will demand most of your time, and maybe you'll not quite achieve that level of conditioning or proficiency required of the world's great climbing challenges. But you'll know they are out there, and as you grasp that high hold at your home crag or in the gym, you can close your eyes for just a moment and be anywhere you wish.

G L O S S A R Y

Note that all cultures have their jargon, most because the terms fit, but some simply to lend exclusivity to the club. Climbing's lexicon is steadily evolving.

AID CLIMBING (a.k.a. ARTIFICIAL CLIMBING) As opposed to *free* climbing, aid climbers rely on gear directly for upward progress instead of using just hands and feet and using the rope only for safety in the event of a fall.

ANCHOR The point at which a rope is fixed at a belay or for a top-rope. Or as a verb, to fix the rope or the climber fast at a belay or top-rope site. "You can anchor at those two bolts over there," or "I lowered off the fixed anchor at the top of the first pitch."

ARETE The sharp edge of an outside corner, as on the outside corner of a building. The term was initially used to describe a glacially-carved mountain ridge, but it has become widely used by rock climbers to describe any outside edge.

ARM BAR A method for climbing a wide crack (see page 44).

BELAY The process by which one manages a rope for a climber. The climber is *on belay* when the belayer is ready to lock off the rope in the event of a fall.

BIG WALL This not-so-precise term is applied to the long climbs (1,000 feet or more), generally those involving bivouacs, aid climbing, and load-hauling.

BIVOUAC A night spent out in the mountains, not at a camp, but out on the climb itself. (a.k.a. *bivy*)

BOLT A rod of metal set into a pre-drilled hole (usually three-eighths of an inch by two inches deep). The carabiner clips to a *hanger*, some kind of ring connected to the bolt.

BUCKET A large, incut handhold.

CAM Anything that widens as it rotates. Spring-loaded devices such as Friends cam or expand as they turn. Climbers also *cam* a foot in a crack by sticking it in on edge and then flattening it out to make it secure.

CARABINER A metal snap link with a variety of uses for climbers.

CHICKEN WING Along with arm bar as a method of climbing a wide crack (see page 44).

CHIMNEY A wide crack (more than a foot) which is ascended by wedging the whole body in and shimmying upwards. The term is also a verb referring to the act of climbing such a crack.

CHOCK Any metal wedging device that is slotted into a crack as an anchor or protection.

CLEAN This has two meanings. As an adjective, it describes climbing a route without transgression by protecting the route without resorting to hammer or drill: "The route is safe with clean gear," or by climbing the route without grabbing or hanging on gear, "After falling a few times, Harry finally got the route clean." As a verb, it refers to the second's job of removing the gear as he follows a leader: "Don't forget to clean that last chock before the traverse."

CORDELETTE A long (approximately 18-foot) length of cord tied into a loop, used among other things, for equalizing belay loads.

CRAG A small cliff.

CRUX The hardest move on a particular climb.

DEADPOINT The moment during a "dynamic" or lunging upward move when the body seems weightless; it's the precise moment when you can move a hand upward to grab another hold before you drop. Using such momentum is generally reserved for experts on hard routes that are well protected.

DIHEDRAL An inside corner formed by two walls of rock, generally at 90 degrees to each other (a.k.a. open book, inside corner).

EDGING Using the edge of a climbing sole to stand on a narrow hold.

FACE CLIMBING Climbing on a smooth expanse of rock using handholds and footholds — as opposed to crack climbing or friction climbing.

FIST CRACK A crack that is too wide for conventional hand jams and which can be ascended by wedging the fist endwise (3- to 4-inch).

FLAKE A slab of rock detached from the main face. Could be tiny as in a finger hold or huge as a 100-foot corner.

FLASH To lead a route successfully on one's first try.

FREE Climbed without directly using gear for upward progress. The rope is used only for safety in the event of a fall.

FRICTION CLIMBING A kind of climbing on low-angle rock where one places as much sole rubber on the rock as possible for purchase. Few climbs are pure *friction*, most involve elements of face climbing as well.

FRIEND The first of many active, spring-loaded camming devices.

HAND JAM Wedging a hand into a crack for purchase.

HEX Short for Hexentric, a six-sided chock made by Black Diamond that uses camming to enhance its wedging action.

JAM OR JAMMING The technique by which fingers or hands or feet (or whatever) are wedged into a crack for purchase.

JUGA Large handhold. Or as a verb, *to jug* is slang for to *jumar*, meaning to ascend a rope with mechanical ascenders like jumars.

JUMAR One of several types of mechanical ascenders.

LAYBACK Or *lieback*. A common technique where the feet are pushed against one surface of rock while the hands pull in the opposite direction. The opposing forces keep the climber on the rock. It is most useful in a 90-degree inside corner, but the principle of opposition applies to almost all climbing moves.

LEAD CLIMBING As opposed to top-rope climbing. A leader starts at the base of the route with no preset safety rope from above. He protects himself by placing or clipping anchors (protection) as he ascends. The length of his potential fall depends on the frequency and soundness of this protection.

MULTI-PITCH A description of a climb that is longer than a rope length and that requires at least one belay point along the way.

NUT Same as chock.

NUT TOOL Any stiff piece of metal (approximately 6 inches long) carried by a second on a lead climb, used to loosen stuck chocks.

OFF-WIDTH OR OFF-SIZE A crack that is too wide to jam and too narrow to chimney. A crack between 6 inches and 18 inches is considered *off-width*, and thus a nightmare to climb.

OVERHANG or *roof*, or *ceiling*, or *'hang*. Any section of the wall that juts abruptly outward.

PITCH The length between belay points on a route. A pitch can't exceed a rope length (usually 165 feet), but it is often much less, dictated mainly by the availability of belay anchors and ledges. Top-rope routes are often less than a half pitch. Routes can involve as many as 30 pitches.

PITON or *pin* or *peg*. The metal spike that is hammered into a crack as an anchor. In the 1970s pitons were replaced by the less destructive chocks as clean climbing revolutionized the sport. Today they are used mainly as fixed pieces, left in place where clean gear won't work, or on aid routes, where cracks are too thin to accept chocks.

PRUSIK A sliding friction knot tied by wrapping a thin cord around a rope. Also the act of ascending a rope using prusik knots.

QUICK DRAWS, or *draws*, are short slings with a carabiner on each end. They are used to clip a rope to a protection bolt or to extend the length of any piece of protection. On a sport route, the leader needs only as many *draws* as there are bolts or pitons.

RAPPEL To descend a stationary rope using any of several friction methods to control rate.

RED POINT To climb a route from the ground up without falling or resting on gear. It implies that there were previous inspections and practice sessions on the route before the final success. *Pink Point* is a variation that means quick draws were already in place.

RUNNER A loop of webbing used to extend protection. Or a term referring to the protection itself: "I went a full forty feet before my first runner."

SEND OR SENT Recent jargon referring to success on a route: "Did you hear that Paula just sent that new 5.12?"

SLAB An inclined surface of rock.

SLING A loop of webbing, a runner.

SMEARING Using the surface area of shoe sole rubber on a slope of rock. As opposed to edging.

SPECTRA One of a host of new super strong fibers used for slings and thin cord.

SPORT CLIMBING Short, usually difficult climbs where the protection, usually bolts, is already in place, and where the focus is on gymnastic movement rather than gear use, judgment, or route-finding.

STATIC Without capacity to move or absorb force. As in a static belay straight from an anchor without the climber's body absorbing shock, or as in static rope that doesn't stretch much and can't be used for leading.

STEMMING Bridging or straddling a corner or a chimney. The climber is held in place by applying force to the opposing walls.

STOPPER The name of Black Diamond's wedge-shaped chocks. Now used loosely to refer to any wedge-shaped chock.

THIRD CLASS A grade assigned to a climb that is hard enough to be hazardous, but that doesn't necessarily need a rope and a belay. Climbers also use the term as a verb, meaning that they are climbing without a rope, even if the route's true grade is much harder: "Joe third-classed that 5.9 over there."

TIPS CRACK A thin crack, barely wide enough to accept finger tips.

TRADITIONAL CLIMBING Refers to all that is not sport climbing: placing one's own gear, attempting a route before climbing or inspecting it on a top-rope.

WIRE Refers to the smaller chocks slung on steel cable: "You can get in a couple good wires before the hard move." As a verb it also means to rehearse moves of a climb until they seem instinctive: "Yeah, it was a hard lead, but he wired it on a top-rope first."

ZIPPER An apt term to describe the action of ripping many pieces of protection as one falls: "She thought the gear was good, but she still *zippered*."

S O U R C E S &

R E S O U R C E S

Included here is a selection of websites, suppliers, and organizations that will be useful as you get into climbing. Advertisements in the magazines *Rock and Ice* and *Climbing*, listed below, will give you almost all the other connections you need.

ONLINE SERVICES (The Internet)

The Internet is a powerful place to get started. There is an enormous amount of information available, but it can mean spending hours sifting through dozens of web sites. For specific information, however, it can't be beat. Most websites, even commercial ones, have useful links for clubs, organizations, and magazines. Remember that things change swiftly on the Net, so all information provided below can only be guaranteed at the time of publication.

www.adventuresports.com—useful climbing directory listing outfitters, gyms, services, and gear; also general information and numerous links to other climbing sites.

www.climb.mountainzone.com—articles, features and essays along with gear news and reviews.

www.climber.org—online community composed of several climbing organizations; lists trips, database of peak climb trip reports, online resources, features, and discussion lists.

www.climbingchannel.com—climbing narrative, news, video clips and message board.

www.8a.nu—rankings of world climbers, photos and training tips.

www.gorp.com—directory fea-
tures climbing destinations, skills, narratives, gear guide with links, photo gallery, books and maps, and climbing related links.

www.newenglandbouldering.com—news, features, online store for gear, books, and videos, links to other sites and message board.

www.rocklist.com—climbing information from all over the world, a huge list of climbing related links and online resources, and an online Climbing Guide.

www.webcrag.com—rock climbing and bouldering guide features monthly videos of hard climbs, medical advice and a climber forum.

MAGAZINES

These two magazines and their web pages will be your best connection to the sport with news, features, technical advice, and equipment reviews. Check these first when you are seeking information as dealers, gear, guides, books, videos, and other climbing connections will all be advertised. Online versions offer additional articles, archived issues, and useful links to retailers, organizations, grants, and other sites of interest to climbers.

CLIMBING
0326 Highway 133
Suite 190
Carbondale, CO 81623
800-493-4569
970-963-9449
www.climbing.com

ROCK AND ICE
5444 Spine Road, Mezzanine A
Boulder, CO 80301
303-499-8410
Fax: 303-530-3729
www.roackandice.com

You can also check out these online climbing magazines:

www.toprope.com—informal, entertaining online magazine.

www.gripped.com—Canadian climbing magazine with guides to climbing in Canada, feature excerpts, and links to climbing resources.

www.highalaska.com—features, environmental alerts, photos, calendar, trip reports, forum.

www.motherrock.com —online version of the Southern California climbing magazine.

www.risk.ru—Risk Journal—a Russian magazine (with an English version) about mountains and expeditions in Asia.

www.rock.com/au—Rock—Australia's climbing magazine.

www.topprope.com—informal, entertaining online magazine.

INSTRUCTION AND GUIDING

There are many good instructors outside of these two listings, but the AMGA and the ACMG each have high standards, both for guide certification and guide service accreditation. They'll provide listings in your area.

AMERICAN MOUNTAIN GUIDES ASSOCIATION (AMGA)
710 10th Street
Suite 101
Golden, CO 80401
303-271-0984
Fax: 303-271-1377
www.amga.com

ASSOCIATION OF CANADIAN MOUNTAIN GUIDES (ACMG)
Box 8341
Canmore, AB T1W 2V1
403-678-2885; fax: 403-609-0070
www.acmg.ca

FINDING AN INDOOR CLIMBING WALL

OUTDOOR INDUSTRY ASSOCIATION
3775 Iris Avenue Suite 5
Boulder, CO 80302
303-444-3353; fax: 303-444-3284
www.outdoorindustry.org
Ask for the Climbing Gym Association for listings in your area.

CLUBS AND ORGANIZATIONS

Climbing organizations serve to educate the public and to protect access to climbing areas. Join and support these good causes.

ACCESS FUND
P.O. Box 17010
Boulder, CO 80308-0100
303-545-6772
Fax: 303-545-6774
www.accessfund.org
This is a vital organization,

working with private owners and governmental agencies to keep climbing areas open to the public —They need your support!

AMERICAN ALPINE CLUB
710 Tenth Street, Suite 100
Golden, CO 80401
303-384-0110
Fax: 303-384-0111
www.americanalpineclub.org
The oldest and most broad-based American climbing organization.

AMERICAN SAFE CLIMBING ASSOCIATION (ASCA)
P.O. Box 1814
Bishop, CA 93515
650-843-1473
www.safeclimbing.org
Dedicated to making the sport safer by replacing unsafe bolts and anchors and by educating climbers about safety.

MOUNTAINEERS
300 Third Avenue West
Seattle, WA 98119
800-573-8484
206-284-6310
Fax: 206-284-4977
www.mountaineers.org
Devoted to exploration and conservation of the outdoors and wilderness areas; sponsors climbing activities and offers courses.

ROCKY MOUNTAIN FIELD INSTITUTE (RMFI)
1520 Alamo Avenue
Colorado Springs, CO 80907
719-471-7736
www.rmfi.org
"Dedicated to the preservation and protection of mountains, crags, and wilderness."

BOOKS
Mountaineering: The Freedom of the Hills, Don Graydon (Editor), et.al. 1997. Paper. $24.95. The Mountaineers.
Considered to be one of the foremost authorities on gear and technique—this is just one of the long line of fine mountaineering books from The Mountaineers

(see address under "Organizations" above.)

The next three books are my favorites from the *How to Climb Series* from Chockstone Press:

Climbing Anchors, John Long. 1993. Paper. $12.95. Chockstone Press.
One of a fine series by John Long, a climbing pioneer and one of the country's best climbing writers.

Knots for Climbers, Craig Luebben. 1995. Paper. $4.95. Chockstone Press.

Self Rescue, David J. Fasulo. 1996. Paper. $12.95. Chocstone Press.
Describes and illustrates a variety of techniques every climber should know to be prepared for a climbing emergency.

BOOK SUPPLIERS

Guidebooks are available to most climbing areas and are too numerous to list here. If the local outdoor supplier can't steer you to the area's guidebook, the suppliers below will probably be able to help.

ADVENTUROUS TRAVELER
102 Lake Street
Burlington, VT 05401
800-282-3963
Fax: 800-677-1821
www.adventuroustraveler.com
Books, videos, and maps on climbing and other active outdoor sports.

CHESSLER BOOKS
P.O. Box 4359
29723 Troutdale Scenic Drive
Evergreen, CO 80437
800-654-8502
303-670-0093
Fax: 303-670-9727
www.chesslerbooks.com
America's largest bookseller of guidebooks, videos and maps, plus new and out-of-print mountaineering books.

VIDEOS

You'll find both high-octane thrillers and sound instructional films from these suppliers:

ADVENTUROUS TRAVELER
(see address under "Book Suppliers".)

CHESSLER BOOKS
(see address above under "Book Suppliers".)

JUST PUSH PLAY
141 Suburban Road
San Luis Obispo, CA 93401
800-727-6689
www.justpushplay.com

ROCK AND ICE
(see address above under "Magazines".)

VIDEO ACTION SPORTS
141 Suburban Rd.
San Luis Obispo, CA 93401
800-727-6689
Fax: 805-541-8544
www.videoactionsports.com

MAIL-ORDER/ONLINE SOURCES OF EQUIPMENT

This is just a sampling of the many mail-order gear suppliers. Check out their online stores or contact for a catalog. Or go to www.climbingmall.com for a list of sources for specific items.

ADVENTURE GEAR
3311 Highway 5, Suite D
Douglasville, GA 30135
888-241-1864
770-577-7722
Fax: 770-577-7744
www.ewalker.com

BACK COUNTRY STORE
2210 South US Hwy 40, Suite C
Heber City, UT 84032
800-409-4502
435-657-2468
www.backcountrystore.com

BLACK DOME MOUNTAIN SPORTS
140 Tunnel Road
Asheville, NC 28805
800-678-2367
828-251-2001
www.blackdome.com

CAMPMOR
810 Route 17 North
P.O. Box 999
Paramus, NJ 07652
888-226-7667
201-445-5000
www.campmor.com

CLIMB AXE, LTD.
2105 SE Division Street
Portland, OR 97202
503-797-1991
www.climbaxe.com

CLIMB HIGH
135 Northside Drive
Shelburne, VT 05482
802-985-5056
Fax: 802-985-9141
www.climbhigh.com

CLIMBERS CHOICE INTERNATIONAL
726 Rossanley Drive
Medford, OR 97501
888-702-3891
541-245-4068
Fax: 541-245-4072
www.climberschoice.com

MOUNTAIN GEAR
730 N. Hamilton
Spokane, WA 99202
800-829-2009
www.mgear.com

MOUNTAIN TOOLS
P.O. Box 222295
Carmel, CA 93922
800-510-2514
Fax: 831-620-0977
www.mtntools.com

PETZL AMERICA
P.O. Box 160447
Freeport Center, Bldg. M7
Clearfield, UT 84016
www.petzl.com

PIKA MOUNTAINEERING
1387 South Roberta Street
Salt Lake City, UT 84115
801-485-1686
Fax: 801-485-0578
www.pikamtn.com

**RAGGED MOUNTAIN
EQUIPMENT**
Box 130, Route 16 & 302
Intervale, NH 03845
603- 356-3042
Fax: 603-356-8815
www.raggedmountain.com

REI
Sumner, WA 98352
800-426-4840
253-891-2500
Fax: 253-891-2523
www.rei.com

**SHORELINE MOUNTAIN
PRODUCTS**
21 Golden Gate Drive #C
San Rafael, CA 94901
800-381-2733
415-455-1000
Fax: 415-455-1363
www.shorelinemtn.com

CLIMBING HOLDS: MANUFACTURERS AND DEALERS

**METOLIUS MOUNTAIN
PRODUCTS**
63189 Nels Anderson Road
Bend, OR 97701
541-382-7585
Fax: 541-382-8531
www.metoliusclimbing.com

NICROS
105 State Street
St. Paul, MN 55107
800-699-1975
www.nicros.com

VOODOO HOLDS
3920 E. Huntington Drive,
Suite D
Flagstaff, AZ 86004
800-883-6433
Fax: 928-526-1007
www.voodooholds.com

CLIMBING WALLS: MANUFACTURERS AND CONSULTANTS

COMP WALL
1072 Folsom Street
Suite 319
San Francisco, CA 94103
415-551-1455
www.compwall.com

EXTRAVERTICAL
61 W. 62nd Street
New York, NY 10023
212-865-4383
Fax: 212-586-5382
www.extravertical.com
Consulting on walls, competitions, programs, etc.

ELDORADO WALL COMPANY
2829 Mapleton Avenue
Boulder, CO 80301
303-447-0512
Fax: 303-447-8356
www.eldowalls.com

ENTREPRISES
20512 Nels Anderson Place
Bend, OR 97701
800-580-5463
www.ep-usa.com

GRIPHEAD
5251 Route 212
Mt. Tremper, NY 12475
914-688-7157
Fax: 914-688-7424
www.griphead.com

NICROS
*(see address under Climbing
Holds)*
651-778-1974

RADWALL
2625 Alacatraz Avenue
Suite 374
Berkeley, CA 94705
510-655-3859
Fax: 510-655-3380
www.radwall.com

SOLID ROCK WALL SYSTEMS
444 Via El Centro
Oceanside, CA 92054
888-355-6566
760-721-3664
Fax: 760-721-3605
www.solidrockwallsystems.com

PHOTO CREDITS

DOUG BERRY/OUTSIDE IMAGES: 42 (top), 159, 162

COURTESY OF BLACK DIAMOND EQUIPMENT: 58 (bottom), 59, 101 (bottom)

JAMIE BLOOMQUIST/OUTSIDE IMAGES: 29

MARK DOOLITTLE/OUTSIDE IMAGES: 128, 129

GREG EPPERSON: 8, 13, 19, 24, 26, 40 (top left & bottom), 42 (bottom), 44 (left), 45, 49, 90, 103, 111, 117, 126, 127, 132, 134, 135, 138, 144, 163, 176, 177

JOHN GOODMAN: 11, 23, 35, 51, 60, 77, 82 (top), 83, 84, 85, 104, 105, 108 (top), 125, 145, 146 (both), 150, 153, 155, 170, 171

JOHN GOODMAN/COURTESY OF CLIMB HIGH: 53, 54, 55, 58 (top), 61, 63, 64, 66, 75, 82 (bottom), 93, 101 (top), 108 (bottom), 109, 133

DANIEL GOODYEAR/NEW MEDIA: 80

KENNAN HARVEY: 12, 39 (bottom right), 95, 166

BRIAN HOLLINGSWORTH: 20, 43 (bottom, both), 44 (right), 46 (top left & bottom), 114

BRIAN HOLLINGSWORTH/TERRY WILD STUDIO: 46 (right)

ACE KVALE: 38 (left), 40 (top right), 50, 67, 149, 158, 173, 174, 178

BECKY LUIGART-STAYNER: 165, 168

MARK MESCHINELI: 92, 151

JIM THORNBURG/OUTSIDE IMAGES: 100

DENNIS TURVILLE: 88

BETH WALD: 15, 16, 21, 25, 31, 32, 36, 37, 38 (right), 39 (left & top right), 41, 43 (top, both), 52, 72, 73, 79, 102, 110, 131, 137, 140, 141, 142, 143, 175

TERRY WILD STUDIO: 113, 118

I N D E X